PARADISE LOST

REASON AND REVELATION IN THE WORKS OF JOHN MILTON

ALEXANDER JACOB

978-1-7638613-6-7

PARADISE LOST
Reason and Revelation in the Works of John Milton

ALEXANDER JACOB

© Manticore Press, Melbourne, Australia, 2025.

All rights reserved, no section of this book may be utilized without permission, except brief quotations, including electronic reproductions without the permission of the copyright holders and publisher. Published in Australia.

MANTICORE PRESS
WWW.MANTICORE.PRESS

CONTENTS

PREFACE 5

INTRODUCTION... 7
The Intellectual Background

CHAPTER 1 15
The Early Works

CHAPTER 2 41
Paradise Lost I

CHAPTER 3 61
Paradise Lost II

CHAPTER 4 85
Paradise Regained

BIBLIOGRAPHY 105

PREFACE

John Milton (1608-1674) will undoubtedly remain one of England's greatest poets but his religion and politics are matters of greater controversy. After obtaining his Master's at Christ College, Cambridge, in 1632, Milton continued his studies privately and undertook extensive travels in Europe from 1638 and 1639. Once returned to England he ventured fervently in support of the Parliamentarian and anti-Episcopal (High Church) cause. Since his 1649 work *The Tenure of Kings and Magistrates* even justified regicide (Charles I was executed in January 1649), he was welcomed into the Republican state in that year as Secretary for Foreign Tongues. Another defence of regicide *Eikonoklastes* (1649) was followed by a *Defensio pro populi anglicano* (1652). His second defence of the English people, *Defensio secunda* (1654) was in praise of Oliver Cromwell, who ruled as Lord Protector from 1653 to 1658. Although Milton became totally blind by 1652 he continued his work as Secretary with the help of assistants until the Restoration of Charles II in 1660. His late Republican writings included *A Treatise of Civil Power* (1659) and the anti-Catholic *Of True Religion* (1672). Though he feared the return of Charles II, he was saved by the royal 'Generall Pardon' of 1660.

Milton's numerous anti-prelatical tracts reveal his deep hatred of hierarchical church organisation and his affinity with the Reformed Christianity movement that is now called Puritanism. One marked feature of Milton's Puritanism that persists in his epic poetical works is his Lutheran-Calvinistic preoccupation with the supreme authority of the Bible. This blind reverence for the 'Book' is indeed similar to the Islamist's veneration of the Quran – though the latter 'Book' is, of course, very different in style from the Hebraic-Christian one that it alludes to. In the case of a distinguished classical scholar like Milton, the total obedience to the Hebrew scriptures leads ineluctably to a deplorable devaluation of classical learning compared to Hebraic as well as to a more general anti-intellectualism. It is this danger that I wished to point to in my 1977 Master's thesis at the School of English, University of Leeds (titled 'Milton's attitude to knowledge'). I am glad to be able to share this thesis today with students of seventeenth century English literature.

    Alexander Jacob
    Toronto, 2025

INTRODUCTION
THE INTELLECTUAL BACKGROUND

One of the strange twists that Milton's Christianity gave to his philosophy was the ultimate transformation of his irascible anti-scholasticism into modes of thought and belief that can be described only as scholastic. In order to determine the nature of this rather paradoxical metamorphosis, we should, I think, consider carefully both the dominant traits of the scholastic method and the violent protests that Milton made against this method in his writings.

An illuminating survey of the origins and trends of seventeenth-century philosophy is offered by Howard Schultz's and Basil Willey's brilliant chapters on 'Traditions of Sobriety' (in *Milton and Forbidden Knowledge*, N.Y., 1955, pp.1-42) and 'The Rejection of Scholasticism' and 'Bacon and the Rehabilitation of Nature' (in *The Seventeenth Century Background*, London, 1934, pp.1-40) respectively. But merely to highlight the paradox I have indicated, I should like here to outline some relevant areas of European philosophical traditions and to suggest also the complexity of the intellectual context in which Milton lived and wrote.

Precepts of intellectual sobriety, as Schultz points out, date back to the classical age itself. Homer, Hesiod,

Aeschylus, Socrates, Pyrrho, Seneca, all in various ways decried intemperate knowledge and commended, instead, the 'ethical science' of self-knowledge. In the early Middle Ages, these warnings against curiosity were usefully adopted by the Christian Fathers and strengthened by quotations from the Scriptures (and especially St. Paul): 'Take heed lest any man spoil you through philosophy and vain deceit', 'The natural man receiveth not the things of the spirit' and 'knowledge puffeth up, but charity edifieth'. In this process of Christianisation, the Socratic theme of 'know thyself' was given a new form by divines like Augustine and Bernard of Clairvaux. Their medieval mode of Christianity, though partly derived from classical precepts, did its best to check classical learning and natural science as unprofitable to the task of self-knowledge. Instead, it insisted on the primacy of human humility, and the attainment, through this humility, of the knowledge of God. Interest in natural phenomena like the 'plurality of worlds' was an 'unchallenged illustration of curiosity' (Schultz); and the Fall of Satan and the Fall of Eve were, in Bernard's opinion, powerful examples of the folly of idle speculations.

In the thirteenth century however, rationalistic and naturalistic philosophy was given a boost with the arrival of Aristotelian literature from Spain and Sicily. Scholastics like Albert Magnus and his pupil Thomas Aquinas put these newly discovered classics to godly use by reinterpreting the Aristotelian system in a Christian idiom, with the blessing of Augustinian Neoplatonism. Even though Aquinas did not accept fully Aristotle's praise of 'rational intuition' as the only instrument capable of comprehending Eternal Forms, he was nevertheless the most rationalist of scholastics. For he believed that the most part of revealed truth was intelligible to and demonstrable by reason. He in effect tried to synthesize philosophy and theology; to use Willey's words,

'In St. Thomas Aquinas, Aristotle is harmonised with Paul and Augustine, metaphysics with revelation, reason with faith'.[1] Yet, in spite of his Baconian attempt to grant reason a certain autonomy under faith, his religious convictions were ultimately stronger than his philosophical interests. And so, in his writings, he constantly stressed faith over reason, since the former gave access to truths not accessible to reason. The main reason for the relative insignificance of Aquinas' position as a thinker in the history of European Rationalism is, therefore, his obligatory Christian acceptance of authority and faith as the starting points from which to build conclusions using reason, whereas the complete rationalistic philosopher relies always, and mainly, on the natural light of reason.

In the fourteenth and fifteenth centuries, Scholastic thinkers, especially Duns Scotus and William of Ockham, moved further away from Aristotelian Rationalism and declared that arguments from effects to causes (i.e. from the world to God) would always be inconclusive. In the late sixteenth and seventeenth centuries, Protestant Scholastics stressed, once again, the importance of reason, but appealed more often to the authority of the Bible in their preoccupation with the dogmatic systems of Luther and Calvin, which had, after the Reformation, become a venerable tradition. This dogmatic trend was to prove fatal to the validity of Protestant Scholasticism in the increasingly Scientific seventeenth century. The "truth" of any proposition in Scholasticism, 'depended ultimately not upon its correspondence with any particular 'state of affairs', but its being consistent with a body of given and of course unquestionable doctrine.[2] In this philosophy of Being (as opposed to a science of Becoming) natural Fact thus lost its

---

[1] Willey, *op cit.*, p.13.

[2] Willey, *op cit.*, p.13.

identity in the greater Metaphysical Truths. The important consideration was not how things behave or what their history might be but how they linked with Total Being.³

This feature of Scholasticism was clearly not conducive to scientific investigation. In fact, as Bacon indicated in *The Advancement of Learning*, the Divines (who were mostly university educated enthusiasts of Scholasticism) objected to learning on several metaphysical, in their case scriptural, grounds: 'I hear (them) say... that the aspiring to overmuch knowledge, was the original temptation and sin, whereupon ensued the fall of man; that knowledge hath in it somewhat of the serpent, and therefore where it entereth into a man it makes him swell, *'scientia inflat'*.⁴ Nature, in general, was considered to be opposed to Divine Grace, and man's happiness depended on his choosing the latter rather than the former as the object of his life's study. (It is, incidentally, interesting that both poetic examples which Willey gives us of Nature's status in medieval Christianity are from Milton.⁵)

This is not to say that all seventeenth-century Scholastics were obscurantists, apart from their religious respect for Reason. Donne for example was a staunch follower of Augustine and his education was almost entirely scholastic. Yet he, like his Bishop John King, exalted learning

---

³ Willey, *op. cit.*, p.15.

⁴ Bacon, *Advancement of Learning*, London 1825, p.7.

I should like here to quote Bacon's reply to this particular problem of the Fall: '*it was not the pure knowledge of nature and universality*, a knowledge by the light whereof man did give names unto other creatures in Paradise, as they were brought before him, according unto their proprieties, which gave occasion to the Fall; *but it was the proud knowledge of good and evil*, with an intent in man to give law unto himself, and to depend no more upon God's commandments, which was the form of temptation', (Bacon, *op. cit.*, p.8), for it may prove illuminating when we consider Milton's treatment of the Fall of Man in *Paradise Lost*. (See my 4th chapter).

⁵ See Willey, *op. cit.*, p.32.

as opposed to 'Popish and Brownist obscurantism' and had nothing but contempt for those who rejected pagan philosophy. In fact, he even resembled the naturalists in defending science, like Bacon, with the Biblical account of Adam naming the animals. The only thing he could not on any account reconcile himself to was, he said, curiosity that betrayed irreverent motives and a desire for useless, devilish knowledge.[6] As a further example of the complexity of Renaissance modes of thought, it should be pointed out that the humanists, who ostensibly deplored the Scholastics' anti-naturalism, were often near-obscurantists. The concern for knowledge related to action rather than knowledge as mere contemplation was, for instance, one of the dangers that Ascham pointed out in contemporary Renaissance thought.[7] Erasmian satire, in particular, came close to annihilating all learning with its numerous destructive criticisms of grammarians, scientists and divines and its insistent reference to man's inferiority to animals. Montaigne too, like Erasmus, preached 'the virtues of self-study and knowing for the sake of doing' (Schultz). But he went somewhat further and maintained that all unnecessary learning would die a natural death when the study of *nature* was properly established.

The climax of this growing mood of naturalism was, as we know, the arrival of Bacon and his scientific appeal for a return to nature. Bacon's philosophy came dangerously close to Erasmus' and Montaigne's in some respects, most notably in his extreme disregard for the scholastic system of 'mind studying mind'. For, 'in sweeping out such cobwebs, Bacon swept out mathematics'. (Schultz, *op. cit.*, p.34). And his

---

[6] See Schultz, *op. cit.*, pp.17-21.
 In fact, I think, Donne provides a good measuring-stick with which to assess the mildness or intensity of Milton's scholastic tendencies.

[7] See Schultz H., *op. cit.*, p.27.

enthusiasm for nature was so great that it led him to extract natural science out of the mythological stories of Proteus, Cupid, Proserpina and the Sphinx! Yet, this anti-rationalism notwithstanding, Bacon did achieve a major intellectual triumph in trying to separate the Truth of Religion from the Truth of Science and, in acknowledging the equal validity of the two scriptures' — God's written word and His created universe. It was this sagacious division that both ensured the approval of a religiously sober scientific age and saved him from what is perhaps the most unfortunate quality of scholastic intellectualism — its use of reason almost solely to explain its preconceived notions of divinity and its stifling subordination of all natural 'facts' to metaphysical 'truths'.

Milton's own sympathies were, apparently at least, with the progressive forces of his age. In the early writings for example, we note an adolescent enthusiasm for free intellectual endeavour that may even be mistaken for a Baconian attitude to knowledge and learning. Of course, there are genuine resemblances between some of Milton's thought and Bacon's. But these are, as I intend to show, mostly incidental and superficial. Like many of his contemporaries, especially Hobbes,[8] Milton was vehemently against the whole concept of scholasticism and so found it additionally convenient to support Bacon against the schoolmen. But a close analysis of the writings will reveal

---

[8] One of Hobbes' chief objections against scholasticism was that 'scholastic explanations not only explain nothing, but discourage further research. They were the explanations of men who felt that all really important truth was already known and were therefore not eager to fill in the picture with physical detail' (Willey, op. cit., p.99). Whether Milton was more Hobbesian or Scholastic in this respect, remains to be seen. One characteristic, however, Milton undeniably shared with Hobbes — for, as Willey says, 'contempt is one of the commonest of Hobbes' emotions: contempt for all upholders of what he calls "Aristotelity," and their doctrines. He is unable to conceive 'that schoolmen and theologians can be anything but madmen and knaves'. (Willey, *op. cit.*, p.95).

that Milton's Baconianism has nothing either of Bacon's cautious dichotomy between science and religion or of his commendation of the senses above reason. On the contrary, we will discover that the increasingly strident note of Christianity in Milton's utterances only betrays his unconscious, but yet very real, affinity with the theologically 'rational' scholastics whom he sought so hard to devastate.

∼

The works I shall consider as illustrations of Milton's peculiar attitude to knowledge are the Second, Sixth and Seventh *Prolusions*, *Of Education*, *Areopagitica*, *Paradise Lost* and *Paradise Regained*. These are by no means the only statements of Milton's intellectual preferences and prejudices. But they are nevertheless the only major discussions of intellectual issues as such, and all the numerous references to related topics in the other prose writings[9] are, in my opinion, incidental echoes of what Milton has asserted in these works.

---

[9] See Samuel, 'Milton on Learning and Wisdom' in *PMLA,* 64i, 1949, pp.708-23, for examples of such references in *The Reason of Church Government, Animadversions, Of Christian Doctrine, Of Reformation, Tetrachordon, Of Prelacy, Defensio, Pro Se Defensio* and *Of Civil Power*.

CHAPTER 1
THE EARLY WORKS

I

Some of the earliest manifestations of Milton's interest in knowledge are to be found in the academic exercises he wrote at Cambridge — the *Prolusions*. The exact significance that one ought to attach to these exercises is difficult to ascertain. H.R. Fletcher's admirably detailed study of the 'Public Discourses' at Cambridge (in *The Intellectual Development of John Milton*, Univ. of Illinois Press, 1961) reveals the arbitrary way in which students were forced to defend or attack themes chosen for them by their tutors:

> There was no self-righteous selection of the good as opposed to the evil, no possibility [sic] of being on the right side of a case and eschewing the wrong aide. Whichever side of a case the student, was assigned he had to present and then defend.[10]

The evidence that Schultz brings forth to show that Milton's defence of learning in the Seventh Prolusion

---

[10] Fletcher, *The Intellectual Development of John Milton*, p.252.

was accidental and in fact contrary to his own desires seems to confirm this point.[11] If, then, the only purpose of these discussions was to train the undergraduates in the art of disputation, does it not seem as though we already have a total negation of the intellectual value that has been placed on these pieces by critics like Samuel and Grace?[12] Nonetheless, I think the total ambiguity into which Fletcher's revelations cast the *Prolusions* — 'What he actually believed to be true was something else' he remarks[13] — obliges us to give these critics the benefit of the doubt until we can know exactly what that 'something else' was. Besides, an examination of the particular emphases with which Milton defends his theme or rejects that of his opponent will be an illuminating exercise, especially as many of these emphases reassert themselves in later writings.

Of these early discussions the 'Third Prolusion' is clearly meant to be a vehement plea for the encouragement of the new 'scientific' philosophy of the seventeenth century against the medieval scholastic methods that still dominated the universities. The virulence with which Milton attacks the system of education evolved from the philosophies of the scholastics shows, even through the obligatory dressing of rhetoric,[14] his extreme contempt of the schoolmen. And views such as:

---

[11] See Schultz, *Milton and Forbidden Knowledge*, New York, pp. 77-80.

[12] See Samuel, 'Milton on Learning and Wisdom' in *PMLA*, '49, p.717 & Grace, *Ideas in Milton*, p.48, for example.

[13] Fletcher, *op. cit.*, p.494.

[14] For the important role of rhetoric in the public disputations see Fletcher *op. cit.*, pp.253-4.

> these useless and barren controversies and bickerings lack all power to affect the emotions in any way whatever; they merely dull and stupefy the intellect.[15]

and

> when I go through these empty quibbles as I often must, against my will, it seems to me as if I were forcing my way through rough and rocky wastes, desolate wildernesses, and precipitous mountain gorges.[16]

are obviously so dear a preoccupation of his mind that they appear, with slight variations, all through his writings. However, Milton's arguments against the scholastics, for all their liveliness, are in the end self-defeating. For the techniques attacked by him are in fact the very same ones that he effectively employs in this and many other works:[17]

> these quick-change philosophasters of ours argue back and forth, one bolstering up his thesis on every side, another labouring hard to cause its downfall, while what one would think firmly established by irrefutable arguments is forthwith shattered by an opponent with the greatest ease.[18]

---

[15] Milton, *Complete Prose Works*, ed. Wolfe and others, Vol. I, p.244.

[16] Op. cit., p.243.

[17] The dialectical method is, for example, employed in a significant way in the dialogue between Comus and the Lady in *Comus*, ll. 665-809 and in the astronomical dialogue in *Paradise Lost*, BK. VIII, ll.1-202.

[18] Milton, *op. cit.*, p.245.

Considering this, the readers may indeed be forgiven if they judge all the negatively critical aspects of Milton's essay in the light of a young student's impatient annoyance with the rigours of the studies he had to undergo at college. And if this view of the destructive passages as products of youthful petulance is true, then the more positive aspects of the work too must perforce be considered with suspicion. The 'enthusiasm' so often pointed out here is really of a kind with the vitriolic blasts that preceded it. Oratorical magnificence such as:

> Now surely divine poetry, by that power with which it is by heavenly grace indued, raises aloft the soul smothered by the dust of earth and sets it among the mansions of heaven, and breathing over it the scent of nectar and bedewing it with ambrosia instile into it heavenly felicity and whispers to it everlasting joy.[19]

This tells us little of any genuine intellectual interest on Milton's part. Instead it shows how Milton here conveniently uses 'the petty triumphs of rhetoric' to escape from the real problems of knowledge that dialectical logic at least attempts, albeit aridly, to sort out. As for the 'Baconian' defence that is only too often erected around Milton's weaknesses, I think it would scarcely do to quote in support of Milton a man who not only admitted that the schoolmen (in spite of the 'contentiousness' of their learning) possessed a 'great thirst of truth'[20] but also had this to say of style:

---

[19] *Op. cit.*, p. 243-4.

[20] Bacon, *op. cit.*, p.41.

> But the excess of this [style] is so justly contemptible, that as Hercules, when he saw the image of Adonis, Venus' minion, in a temple, said in disdain "Nil sacries": so there is none of Hercules' followers in learning that is, the more severe and laborious sort of inquirers into truth, but will despise those delicacies and affectations, as indeed capable of no divineness.[21]

Nevertheless, the conclusion of this Prolusion is remarkable in one respect. The range of knowledge recommended by Milton here is virtually boundless, 'not ... bounded and cabined by the limits which encompass the earth',[22] and the religious promptings of his nature were apparently not yet loud enough to condemn the mind's need to 'wander beyond the confines of the world'[23] as immoral. However it is significant that even in this early Prolusion, we are firmly reminded that 'the supreme purpose of all sciences' is 'the general good' and 'the honour and profit of our country'.[24]

Milton's Second Prolusion 'On the Harmony of the Spheres' may seem at first glance to represent a youthful interest in astronomical subjects that was soured by the time he wrote the famous dialogue on astronomy in the Eighth Book of *Paradise Lost*.[25] But a closer reading of this oration

---

[21] *Ibid.*, p.38.

[22] Milton, *op. cit.*, p.247.

[23] *Op. cit.*, p.247.

[24] *Op. cit.*, p.246.

[25] Fletcher of course goes to the extreme of saying that this Prolusion should not be taken seriously at all since Milton was not an active participant in the discourse but only a jocular herald of it (see Fletcher, *op. cit.*, p.467). This hardly takes account of the fact that Milton, even

will reveal to us that there is nothing scientific at all in his views on celestial music. At the beginning of the work he intelligently suggests that what Pythagoras held was not a literal but rather a figurative, or poetic, notion of '*musica mundana*'. But in the course of defending Pythagoras against Aristotle's literalism, Milton becomes so 'enthusiastic' that he tries to prove Pythagoras' theory on a literal level too. And to do this he conjures up a scriptural-moral explanation (of a Christian as much as of a classical kind) for man's physical inability to hear the supreme harmony. In this irrational mixture of natural phenomenon and religious myth we have a harbinger of the more serious problems of Milton's larger works.[26]

The last of Milton's *Prolusions* and the one most directly relevant to our enquiry is the Seventh, entitled 'Learning brings more blessings than Ignorance'. This last oration delivered at Cambridge is commonly accepted at face value and so appears to be an obvious proof of the young Milton's trust in the powers of the intellect. But, as Schultz has so convincingly shown us the original intention of the author had almost certainly been to defend the opposite side of the debate, in a way suggested to him by his reading of Charron's *De La Sagesse*.[27] may seem another shattering blow to the supporters of Milton's early 'optimism'. But to be fair to them, it must be pointed out that the ignorance that Milton wished originally to defend was not *all* ignorance but that which he,here, ostensibly criticised as 'Socrates' famous ignorance'

---

though merely introducing the topic of debate, markedly leans toward the Pythagorean theory and thus reveals a genuine personal interest in the subject at hand.

[26] This mixture also, I think, reflects the worst of Baconian naturalism. See my Introduction, p.6.

[27] Schultz, *op. cit.*, p.78.

and 'the Sceptics' timid suspension of judgement'.[28] And as Socratic self-knowledge and a sceptical use of right 'reason' were anyway concomitant with learning at all stages of the 'evolution' of Milton's ideas on learning, this evidence of Schultz's alone should not detract greatly from the argument of those who claim to detect a quite positive intellectualism in the early Milton.

If, on the other hand, Schultz's theory is by some unlikely chance found to be invalid and all we are left with once again is the ambiguity of Fletcher's findings, this Prolusion too no doubt deserves a careful analysis. The learning that Milton encourages here is again literally limitless. In one bristling passage ('Moreover if this human happiness ... Governor'),[29] he describes the thrills of a universal knowledge in a manner that is surely comparable with that of the most fervent, scientific literature of the Renaissance. The language used here is indeed so purely humanistic that Milton even seems to risk sacrilege for a moment by attributing to the learned man a power 'equal to that of the Gods themselves'. Here it seems we have a rare instance of intellectual ardour that is quite untainted by ulterior motives of an overtly religious-utilitarian sort. When Milton exclaims:

> What a thing it is to grasp the nature of the whole firmament and of its stars, all the movements and changes of the atmosphere, ...[30]

we cannot but get the impression of one who is indeed hungry for knowledge for the sake of knowledge itself!

---

[28] Even in Charron's dissertation we find it is not ignorance but the judgement and the will that are esteemed above learning.

[29] Milton, *op. cit.*, pp.295-6

[30] *Ibid.*

Unfortunately it is not possible to study this passage apart from its context, and a fuller perusal of this context will reveal not only a rather strict utilitarianism that is allied to his earlier anti-scholastic attitudes, but also a tentative attempt to link knowledge with God that was soon to become an obsession. Whetting our eagerness to embark on the voyage of learning, Milton cautions us against wasting our time on 'useless knowledge': 'This voyage too, will be much shortened if we know how to select branches of learning that are *useful* and what is *useful* within them"[31] (my italics). This gives him another good opportunity to attack the scholastic systems of his teachers and their strange interest in 'thorns and thistles'! His scheme of learning, Milton finally declares, will make sure to 'rule out of every art what is irrelevant, superfluous, or unprofitable' — and we realize that all the earlier craving for knowledge was not quite a paean to the scientific method, but just another extravagant effort to illustrate the current belief (inspired by Baconianism, no doubt) that the end of learning is (in Irene Samuel's words) 'some more perfect management of life'.[32]

The Christian colouring of his logic, however, leads to more dangerous confusions, such as when he asks, 'Do we perceive no purpose in the luxuriance of fruit and herb beyond the short-lived beauty of verdure?'[33] This question may be more simply rephrased as 'Why should there be a luxuriance of fruit and herb?' and we see that Milton is again as guilty of scholasticism as the scholastics he so despises. For, was it not the great triumph of the experimental scientists (whose champion Milton believed himself to be) to replace the 'why' of the scholastics with their own 'how'?

---

[31] *Op. cit.*, p.300.

[32] Samuel, *op. cit.*, p.722.

[33] Milton, *op. cit.*, p.292.

Needless to add, if it were to be asked of every scientific discovery whether it had any religious-moral *raison d'être* or not, we should soon find ourselves 'likely to weep and wail' not because there are no more worlds for us to conquer, but because we know there are other worlds which our various religions will not let us conquer.

Thus, even if we grant more importance to these Prolusions than Schultz was prepared to when he declared 'An academic oration would be slight support for a conclusion so weighty (that the seventh Prolusion marks the most optimistic stage of Milton's evolution)',[34] we find that the intellect hardly features anywhere as a prime concern in itself but is always allied through the convenient link of Baconianism? — to a strict utilitarianism that will ultimately force it to serve the interests of morality and religion.

II

The tractate *Of Education* deserves our attention because it is another of the works supposedly produced out of the abundance of Milton's early 'optimism'. The vast array of classical authors represented in this thesis, along with the generous listing of subjects to be pursued by Milton's ideal students appears a convincing enough proof of Renaissance liberality and love of knowledge. But a consideration of the motives and aims which inspired this tract, as well as of the contents themselves, will, I think, prompt us to be somewhat less extravagant in our praise of Milton's 'faith' in secular learning.

---

[34] Schultz, *op. cit.* p.77.

The immediate reason for the writing of this letter has already been conclusively traced to the Comenian System of education which Hartlib, as a follower, sought to propagandize.[35] Milton, writing as a Baconian against the traditional scholastic regimens of the universities, apparently saw the opportunity to criticise Comenianism as well here. So that, like so much of his prose writings, this letter too was engendered as much by a negative anger as by a positive desire to spread intellectual reform. I am aware that the two motives are not entirely opposed to each other. But by now we should be sufficiently conscious of the dangers of mixing science with polemics to recognize the importance of reminding ourselves that Milton's concern for learning was not now (or indeed ever!) that of a disinterested scholar or philosopher.

The strident tone of anger is witnessed all through the letter. The scholastics come in for the usual debunking in passages like:

> And for the usual method of teaching Arts, I deem it to be an old error of universities not yet well recovered from the Scholastic grossness of barbarous ages, that instead of beginning with Arts most easy, and those be such as are most obvious to the sense, they present their young unmatriculated novices at first coming with the most intellective abstractions of Logic and Metaphysics.[36]

And:

---

[35] See E. Sirluck's Chapter 'Of Educ' in Intro. to Milton, *Complete Prose Works*, ed. Wolfe and others, Vol. II, p. 184ff.

[36] Milton *op. cit*. p.374.

> I doubt not but ye shall have more ado to drive our dullest and laziest youth, our stocks and stubs from the infinite desire of such a happy nurture, than we have now to hale and drag our choisest and hopefullest wits to that asinine feast of sowthistles and brambles which is commonly set before them, as all the food and entertainment of their tenderest and most docile age.[37]

The Comenian principle of *vocational* education is more subtly scathed in the incidental attacks on the 'ambitious and mercenary' men who use their education to ruthlessly further their professions:

> Some allur'd to the trade of Law, grounding their purposes not on the prudent, and heavenly contemplation of justice and equity which was never taught them, but on the promising and pleasing thoughts of litigious terms, fat contentions and flowing fees; others betake them to state affairs, with souls so unprincipl'd in virtue and true generous breeding, that flattery, and court shifts and tyrannous aphorisms appear to them the highest points of wisdom; instilling their barren hearts with a conscientious slavery, if, as I rather think, it be not feind.[38]

More blatant, even obtrusive, is the way in which Milton uses his essay to chastise the government for their lack of character in both civil and martial matters!

---

[37] *Op. cit.*, pp.376-377.

[38] *Op. cit.* p.375.

> They (the students) would not then, if they were trusted with fair and hopeful armies, suffer them for want of just and wise discipline to shed away from about them like sick feathers, though they be never so oft suppli'd; they would not suffer their empty and unrecruitable colonels of twenty men in a company, to quaff out, or to convey into secret hoards, the wages of a delusive list, and a miserable remnant; yet in the meanwhile to be overmaster'd with a score or two of drunkards, the only soldiery left about, them, or else to comply with all rapines and violences.[39]

If the motives involved in writing this letter are not immaculately indicative of intellectualism, the goals which Milton sets his students are even less so. In discussing Milton's aims as an educator, we find ourselves grappling with what appears to be the religious sobriety of the Renaissance. 'The end then of learning is to repair the ruins of our first parents by regaining to know God aright', says Milton even at the beginning of his project. And by the time we reach the end of the tractate we are told that what he has been proposing hitherto is the 'purity of Christian knowledge.' Here, Milton is, like many of his contemporaries, advocating the widespread implementation of Right Reason in our daily affairs. But it remains to be seen whether Milton's conformity to this seventeenth-century (especially Cambridge Platonic) attitude of 'intellectual religion' leads him into limited, unscientific, educational methods or not.

It is interesting to note that, in recognizing our present position in the tangible world 'because our understanding cannot in this body found itself but on sensible things',

---

[39] *Op. cit.* p.412.

Milton shows himself sometimes to be rather too unmindful of his original religious purposes. Before he actually conducts us to the hillside where 'I will point ye out the right path of a virtuous and noble Education' for example, we notice that he defines 'a compleat and generous Education' as 'that which fits a man to perform justly, skilfully and magnanimously all the offices both private and public of peace and war.'[40] And in the catalogue of exercises that Milton outlines in the second section of his work, we find not a list of hymns to be sung regularly as reminders of the ultimate aim of education, but rather a number of war-like sports including sword-fighting and wrestling! The extraordinary importance Milton gives to physical training and the defence of the land is doubtless an indication of the Renaissance interest in patriotism. More importantly, it may be a proof of the Christian humanists' curious ability to assimilate the most worldly considerations into a plan for salvation. So that, instead of being amused like Sensabaugh when he declared:

> If Milton believed such a program would repair the ruins of our first parents, he set up a curious schedule; his academy would be more likely to produce a Sir Philip Sidney than a Saint Augustine or a Saint Francis of Assisi,[41]

we should rather try to read the entire essay in the context of Renaissance education in general, which saw no inherent sin in worldly learning and preparation as long as the

---

[40] Sensabaugh, 'Milton on Learning' in *SP* 43, (1946), p.263.

[41] This feature of Renaissance education is clearly an extension of the medieval method of bending all learning, including such pagan philosophy as was not explicitly 'immoral', to the purposes of Christian Faith. (See my Introduction, p.2, for instance).

educationist could finally manage to reconcile them to Christian ends, as Milton did in his letter:

> These ways would trie all their peculiar gifts of nature and if there were any secret excellence among them, would fetch it out and give it fair opportunities to advance itself by, which could not but mightily redound to the good of this nation, and bring into fashion again those old admired virtues and excellencies, with far more advantage now in this purity of Christian knowledge.[42]

It is fitting to consider at this juncture and in this context, the great display of classical knowledge which is customarily summoned to prove Milton's generous trust in the value of heathen learning. The first references to the Greeks and Latins are to 'Cebes, Plutarch and other Socratic discourses' and 'the two or three first books of Quintilian'. These books of Education may be 'easy and delightful' but, like all the other classics to follow, they have a specific moral purpose to implement in this case, to 'lead and draw (the pupils) in willing obedience, enflamed with the study of learning, and the admiration of virtue, stirr'd up with high hopes of living to be brave men, and worthy patriots, dear to God and famous to all ages'.[43]

Then 'Cato Varro and Columella' are to be read in order to 'improve the tillage of their country, to recover the bad soil and to remedy the waste that is made of good'![44] It is particularly interesting to note that the study of 'natural philosophy', based on 'the Historical Physiology of Aristotle

---

[42] Milton, *op. cit.*, p.413.

[43] *Op. cit.*, p.385.

[44] *Op cit.*, p.389.

and Theophrastus' and Vitruvius and Seneca's 'Natural Questions' and Mala, Celsus, Pliny and Solinus, is to begin with the History of Meteors and end quite definitely with Anatomy. For the student of science must, according to him, finally serve his nation as a physician to himself, his friends and his Army. Here I should like to remind the reader that even Bacon, though generally a 'utilitarian' scientist had once cautioned against 'the over early and peremptory reduction of knowledge into arts and methods; from which time commonly sciences receive small or no augmentation'.[45]

Milton's survey of subjects continues with Ethics, which, not surprisingly, is of greater significance than those kinds of knowledge listed before, and is to be learnt when the student is more mature. For this purpose, the reading of Plato, Xenophon, Cicero, Plutarch, Laestius and 'those Lacrian remnants' is suggested along with David, Solomon, the Evangels and the Apostolic Scriptures. As for the grounds of law, the students are firmly advised to learn them 'with just and with best warrant' from Moses — and then, only 'as far as human prudence can be trusted', from the Grecian, Roman and English laws. In the last stage of their education the students are to undertake a close scrutiny of classical rhetoric, poetry and drama so that, after a simultaneous examination of the *Poetics*, they may finally realize what 'Religious, what glorious and magnificent use might be made of poetry'.[46]

This blend of classical and scriptural learning is believed by Milton to be capable of making the students able writers, speakers and preachers. That Milton was, thus, confident of the virtue of some of the classics 'as an aid to good Christian Renaissance living' cannot be denied. But that does not preclude the fact that the 'universal insight

---

[45] Bacon, *op. cit.*, p.48.

[46] Milton, *op. cit.* p.405.

into things' which he wishes his pupils to be 'fraught' with, must necessarily be a superficial one; Milton's entire scheme of learning is too utilitarian to possess any real value for the intellectual who wishes to use the classics (especially the Rational works of Aristotle and Plato) to learn more ways of seeking more knowledge for a more satisfactory understanding of things. This class of students, Milton does not so much as mention in his treatise, obviously considering them as hateful 'curiosi'. His main concern is with the production of versatile Renaissance gentlemen who would be wise and courtly in war as in peace, and never forget that at the end of all their varied learning they ought somehow to regain 'to know God aright'. We thus see in this letter that the classics, though not yet forbidden, are hardly recognized for their intellectual value but are, instead, constantly subjected to the ethical demands of this ready, 'sober', cure for current educational evils given by one angry 'Baconian' Christian to another somewhat less 'Baconian' than himself.

III

What of a work like *Areopagitica* then? Has not this speech in protest against the new licensing policies of the government been hailed in unequivocal terms by some of the most critical of Milton's modern critics as 'the clearest summons to intellectual freedom and progress'[47] containing a hope of reformation in England that completely overshadowed the Christian vision of the

---

[47] Schultz, *op. cit.* p.193.

city of God?⁴⁸ Was Milton in 1644 really so flushed with an enthusiasm for secular education and the spirit of free intellectual inquiry that he quite forgot his growing religious concerns?

The rhetorical flourishes with which Milton opens his speech bear some encouraging signs, such as his announcement that he intends to show his readers that the new censorship 'will be primely to the discouragement of all learning and the stop of Truth'.[49] In the very next paragraph, though, he is careful to qualify his statement with an announcement that the 'reason' he is defending is not pure 'reason' but in fact the image of God:

> Who kills a Man kills a reasonable creature, God's Image; but he who destroyes a good Booke, kills reason it selfe, kills the Image of God, as it were in the eye.[50]

That this qualification is elaborated, rather than skipped over (as Sensabaugh's remarks suggest) during the development of the oration will be seen by studying the rest of the work.

The means Milton employs to refute his enemies' ideas is now, as always, to pad out his own views with a splendid collection of classical authorities all supposedly in sympathy with himself. We recognize this rhetorical device as a favourite, harmless one dating back to his Cambridge days, and so must take care once again not to attach too much significance to Milton's list of Greek and Roman

---

[48] Sensabaugh, *op. cit.* p.264.

[49] Milton, *op. cit.* p.491.

[50] *Op.cit.* p.492.

thinkers as a proof of extraordinary intellectual ardour. Having said that, it is important to point out that there is one interesting feature in all this sumptuous evidence that Milton calls forth from the classical age to show his readers that licensing was never, in vogue (except within religious limits, to be sure) in those learned days. Here, unlike in *Of Education,* Milton does not subject all these books and authors to a definite utilitarian end. At least so far in the work then, unlimited learning is recommended-perhaps not exactly for a scientific search after Truth, but then also not explicitly for any of the mundane purposes so neatly outlined in the letter to Hartlib.[51]

By the time he comes to the Christian epoch of his historical background however, the polemical nature of this piece too becomes clear. And all the invective that he chooses to pour on the pathetic Popes of Rome and the papified prelates of England, (op. cit., pp.501-507) only helps to rob his own 'liberal' arguments of conviction. For, in spite of all his verbal 'enthusiasm', Milton himself is really labouring under a mental censorship that will not suffer 'any intellectual offspring' that is a 'Monster' (that is, an anti-Protestant entity) to live:

> that also which is impious or evil absolutely either against faith or manners no law can possibly permit.[52]

---

[51] If Milton, in this work, is not particularly a Renaissance 'utilitarian', he is still something of a medieval scholastic. For when later on he refers approvingly to the two Apollinarii 'Fain as a man may say to coin all the seven liberall sciences out of the Bible' (op. cit., p.509) and to Basil teaching 'how some good use may be made of Margites' (*op. cit.*, p.510) he betrays an unconscious affinity with the medieval scholastic systems of extracting all the sciences from the Bible and of permitting for study such heathen literature as was suitable to their Christian purposes.

[52] *Op. cit.*, p.565.

And:

> I mean not tolerated Popery, and open superstition, which as it extirpates all religious and civil supremacies, so it self should be extirpate.[53]

If Milton, in this work, is not particularly a Renaissance 'utilitarian', he is still something of a medieval scholastic. For when later on he refers approvingly to the two Apollinarii 'Fain as a man may say to coin all the seven liberall sciences out of the Bible' (*op. cit.*, p.509) and to Basil teaching 'how some good use may be made of Margites' (*op. cit.*, p.510) he betrays an unconscious affinity with the medieval scholastic systems of extracting all the sciences from the Bible and of permitting for study such heathen literature as was suitable to their Christian purposes.

As Sirluck has pointed out in his Introduction (see Milton, *op. cit.*, p.179), these are the limits on the 'left' and on the 'right' of Milton's tolerationist policies. Even Sirluck, in appreciating the generosity of Milton's intention of tolerating 'indifferences', concedes that 'Milton is more severe than was tactically necessary. Some who denied Roman Catholics the public practice of their religion nevertheless forbade the magistrate to inquire into their consciences'. The reason for this extraordinary strictness with regard to the Papists is that, as Sirluck suggests, the Roman Catholics refused to recognize the unique authority of the Scriptures 'in matters of religion' and instead raised their own man-made institution of the Church as a surrogate guide to the discovery of Truth:

---

[53] *Ibid.*

> The truth Milton gives thanks for ... is that in matters of religion, Scripture is absolutely and solely authoritative ... But he thought it the essence of Roman Catholicism to deny this proposition.[54]

This observation is I think shrewd and, for the most part, accurate. But one feature Sirluck fails to highlight is Milton's use of the word 'truth' in such a cleverly ambiguous way as to belie Sirluck's qualification about 'matters of religion'.

In the beginning of Milton's last argument — that licensing will cause 'the greatest discouragement and affront that can be offered to learning and to learned men', — he stirringly appeals to 'not the mercenary crew of false pretenders to learning, but the free and ingenuous sort of such as evidently were born to study, and love learning for itself, not for lucre, or any other end, but the service of God and of truth'.[55] The curious feature of this statement is that it smoothly equates 'learning for itself' to 'learning for the service of God and of truth', though the former is a markedly intellectualist view of truth and the latter, as we know, a potentially Protestant one. After various betrayals of extreme personal pique[56] that are one of the typically Miltonic weaknesses of this work:

> What advantage is it to be a man over it is to be a boy at school, if he have only scapt the ferula, to come under the fescu of an Imprimatur? If serious and elaborate writings, as if they were no

---

[54] Sirluck in Milton, *op. cit.*, p.181.

[55] Milton, *op. cit.*, p.531.

[56] Both *Of Education* and *The Judgement of Martin Bucer* had been licensed a few months before the writing of *Areopagitica*.

> more than the theme of a grammar lad under his pedagogue must not be uttered without the cursory eyes of a temporizing and extemporizing licenser.[57]

And,

> if in this the most consummat act of his fidelity and ripenesse, no years, no industry, no former proof of his abilities can bring him to that state of maturity, as not to be still mistrusted and suspected, unlesse he carry all his considerat diligence, all his midnight watchings, and expence of Palladian oyl, to the hasty view of an uncensur'd licencer, perhaps much his younger, perhaps far his inferiour in judgement, perhaps one who never knew the labour of book-writing, and if he be not repulst, or slighted, must appear in Print like a punie with his guardian, and his censors hand on the back of his title to be his bayl and surety, that he is no idiot, or seducer, it cannot be but a dishonor and derogation to the author, to the book, to the priviledge and dignity of Learning.[58]

He goes on to develop his argument on a national level:

> And as it is a particular disesteem of every knowing person alive, and most infurious to the writt'n labours and monuments of the dead, so

---

[57] *Op. cit.* p.531.

[58] *Op. cit.*, p.532.

> to me it seems an undervaluing and vilifying of the whole Nation.[59]

In doing so, he starts with generalised references to 'Truth and understanding' and 'all the knowledge in the land' and 'those who had prepar'd their minds and studies above the vulgar pitch to advance truth in others'. But the 'liberality' apparent in the examples he gives us in this section — 'the glory of Italian wits' (op. cit., p.538) and the scientific endeavours of Galileo against the Inquisition is in fact dangerously vulnerable owing to Milton's equivocal notion of truth. For when a little later on he tries to point out the way to 'Truth' through 'forbidden writing' (op. cit., p.542) he skilfully[60] turns his argument to a discussion of purely scriptural truths. And all the following commendations of intellectual debate:

> A man may be a heretick in the truth; and if he believes things only because his Pastor says so or the Assembly so determines without knowing other reason, though his belief be true, yet the very truth he holds, becomes his heresie.[61]

And:

> For if we be sure we are in the right and do not hold the truth guiltily ... what can be more fair, than when a man judicious, learned, and of a conscience, for ought we know, as good as theirs

---

[59] *Op. cit.*, p.535.

[60] I say skilfully because his context here — the problem of 'sects and schisms' — actually warrants this change of focus.

[61] *Op. cit.*, p.543.

that taught us what we know, shall not privily from house to house, which is more dangerous, but openly by writing publish to the world what his opinion is, what his reasons, and wherefore that which is now thought cannot be sound.[62]

Though seemingly very progressive, are all directed towards an ambiguously conceived 'Truth'.

This ambiguity is somewhat clarified when, further on, Milton addresses the Lords and Commons of England as governors of 'a Nation not slow and dull ... not beneath the reach of any point the highest that human capacity can soar to.'[63] He begins by celebrating the 'Old Philosophy of this Island' (interestingly, we note here a tendency to deny the 'writers of antiquity' their originality which will in fact be further developed in *Paradise Regained* Bk. IV[64]). But he soon shifts his attention to this nation's role as 'the first tidings and trumpet of Reformation'. And the rest of this rhetorical section on beholding 'this Vast City' (p.553 ff), is not as Sensabaugh declares, a description of 'a city of Man' that 'completely overshadowed the Christian vision of the City of God'[65] but rather a concretization of Milton's religious views of truth and knowledge. Although full of enthusiastic' admiration (in the manner of the Seventh Prolusion) for 'a Nation so pliant and so prone to seek after knowledge', coloured with the usual classical references: ('The Temple of Janus with his two controversal faces might now not unsignificantly be set open') and flavoured with a less familiar touch of sycophancy ('We can grow ignorant

---

[62] *Op. cit.*, p.547.

[63] *Op. cit.*, p.551.

[64] See my 4th chapter.

[65] Sensabaugh, *op. cit.*, p.264.

again, brutish, formal and slavish, as ye found us; but you [the Lorde and Commons] then must first become that which ye cannot be, oppressive, arbitrary, and tyrannous, as they were from whom ye have free'd us.'), these effusively poetic passages point clearly to the very Christian nature of the 'general reforming' that Hilton hopes for. The whole kingdom, he finally says,[66] is to be 'shaken by God and the 'men of rare abilities' are all to be directed in their 'discovery of truth' by His 'enlightning'!

Before concluding this study of the intellectual aspects of *Areopagitica*, I should like to address myself to some remarks that Sirluck makes about Milton's use of reason above the authority of Scripture and the 'primitive fathers':

> The primary function of these citations (from prophets, apostles and fathers) is to free the issue from the influence of miscellaneous Christian authorities... The 'authority' of one primitive father is opposed to that of another in such a way as to prevent either from being decisive and hence the way is cleared for submitting the issue to the test of reason alone... It is true that the principle is itself introduced by citations from the Scripture, but only in order to prepare a favorable atmosphere for its reception, not as establishing its authority.[67]

This may be so, but it still says very little, positively, of Milton's opinion of the power and uses of reason. Reason is for Milton not an instrument with which to acquire all the 'knowledge' he so craves for the whole nation, but

---

[66] *Op. cit.*, p.566.

[67] Sirluck in Milton, *op. cit.*, pp. 164-5.

rather a means of choosing between moral books and immoral ones:

> For those actions which enter into a man, rather then issue out of him, and therefore defile not, God uses not to captivat under a perpetuall childhood of prescription, but trusts him with the gift of reason to be his own chooser.[68]

The narrow use of reason evidenced in this passage clearly indicates the predominantly ethical quality of the whole of Milton's speech for the liberty of 'unlicens'd printing'. Besides, it also heralds the ambiguous conception of Knowledge and Truth which we have already noticed in the course of our study.

That this ambiguity is, as we have seen, finally resolved in terms of plainly Protestant-nationalistic realities is at once the strength and the bane of this work. Addressing as it does a near-Puritanical Long Parliament, Milton's speech possesses a great persuasive, rhetorical force. But to the reader who seeks proofs of some intellectualism in what has been called Milton's 'organon of progress' (Schultz) it must necessarily be a disappointment. Milton is, here, far from being really concerned with the freedom required for all truly intellectual endeavours. Knowledge and Truth are for Milton an almost entirely Christian affair, and reason, if at all used in the discovery of truth, is to play not the leading role but, rather, the secondary, moral, one of distinguishing the really Christian from the not-so-, or almost falsely, or anti-Christian. For his main interest — in all the works we have so far considered is the proper establishment of Protestantism and Protestant education in England, and the

---

[68] Milton, *op. cit.*, p.513.

destruction of anything that even remotely seems to threaten its security — be it the boogeyman of scholasticism or the more real menace of prelacy, As for the so-called 'optimistic faith' in classical learning, we have seen that Milton's use of the classics in all these early writings has been mostly incidental and wholly subject to the superior demands of Christian Doctrine.

CHAPTER 2
PARADISE LOST I

Bearing in mind the intellectual attitudes revealed in Milton's early works, let us now consider one of his later discussions of the value of intellectual endeavour — the dialogue on astronomy in Bk. VIII of *Paradise Lost*.

Though a dialogue, there are in fact three important characters involved in the proceedings of this absorbing scene. The first of these figures, God, does not actually appear during the conversation in Paradise; but his instructions to Raphael (given earlier on in Bk. V) are nevertheless an important point of reference for us, the audience. The reason why God sends Raphael down to earth, Milton tells us in the Argument of Bk. V, is 'to admonish (Adam) of his obedience, of his free estate, of his enemy near at hand, who he is and why his enemy and whatever else may avail Adam to know'.[69] In God's advice to Raphael 11.224-245 the aims of the angel's conversation are more elaborately specified:

> Such discourse bring on,
> As may advise him of his happy state.
> Happiness in his power left free to will,

---

[69] Milton, *Paradise Lost*, ed.by A. Fowler (Longmans, 1971), p.256.

> Left to his own free will, his will though free,
> Yet mutable; whence warn him to beware
> He swerve not too secure; tell him withal
> His danger, and from whom, what enemy
> Late fallen himself from heaven, is plotting now
> The fall of others from like state of bliss;
> By violence, no, for that shall be withstood,
> But by deceit and lies; this let him know,
> Lest wilfully transgressing he pretend
> Surprised, unadmonished, unforewarned. (V, 233-45)

What God wishes Adam to know is that he is happy in his present condition, that his happiness is nevertheless vulnerable and that he ought therefore to guard against complacency. Also, Adam is to be warned of the exact nature of his enemy and of the way in which that enemy will attack him. Of course, all these warnings are to be relayed to him only in order that Adam will not be able to plead ignorance as an excuse for his fall. It is interesting to note that the actual instructions given by God follow closely Milton's outline of it in his synopsis except in the last injunction which categorically limits Raphael's speech ('this let him know'), whereas Milton in the Argument permits 'whatever else may avail to know'. Either this extra 'whatever else' should be equated to the details of Satan's evil tactics given in lines 242-3, or else it should be explained away as an afterthought which Milton added on to his Argument after he had composed the Book and noticed the difference between God's advice and Raphael's own turns of conversation. In either case, it will be observed that Raphael's speech is somewhat more garrulous than God commanded it to be when, in Bk. V, He 'fulfilled all justice'.

One of the reasons why Raphael's conversation extends over four books of this epic is that he is led on cleverly by Adam into answering an assortment of questions that have little direct connection with the tremendous tragedy to come. Adam's extremely cunning methods of prolonging conversation with Raphael make him appear like a genuine 'curious willing' to go to any lengths of cajolery in the pursuit of knowledge. His first tentative prod at Raphael when it occurs to him 'not to let the occasion pass given him by this great conference to know of things above his world' (V, 453-455) is, for instance, made in an artfully casual way:

> Inhabitant with God, now know I well
> Thy favour, in this honour done to man,
> Under whose lowly roof thou has vouchsafed
> To enter, and these earthly fruits to taste,
> Food not of angels, yet accepted so,
> As that more willingly thou couldst not seem
> At heaven's high feasts to have fed: yet what compare? (V, 11.461-467)

And though, at the end of Raphael's speech, he declares that he is satisfied with the answer, he seems more intent on asking him further questions than on seriously reflecting on the lessons to be drawn from this answer:

> Thy words
> Attentive, and with more delighted ear,
> Divine instructor, I have heard, than when
> Cherubic songs by night from neighbouring hills
> Aerial music send: nor knew I not
> To be both will and deed created free;
> Yet that we never shall forget to love

> Our maker, and obey him whose command
> Single, is yet so just, my constant thoughts
> Assured me, and still assure: though what thou tell'st
> Hath passed in heaven, some doubt within me more,
> But more desire to hear, if thou consent
> The full relation, which must needs be strange,
> (V, 1 544-556).

This typical passage shows us how Adam gently urges Raphael on with flattery and with the disarming ruse of wanting to enjoy the 'high power' of the angelic presence until nightfall. Apparently then curiosity was a normal characteristic of the pre-lapsarian mind. And though Milton may wish to condone it ('and now led on yet sinless with desire to know' Milton says of Adam's questioning in Bk. VII, 60-61) because it is not yet overtly critical of God's works, there is no denying that the innocent Adam is in no way free from the natural thirst for knowledge Milton and so many of his contemporaries considered a potential threat to the spiritual welfare of mankind.[70] Adam's inquiring instincts are greatly encouraged by Raphael's curious uncertainties. (It seems highly strange that God should have chosen as his messenger one so perplexingly ignorant of divine designs!) When for instance, Adam has persuaded him to relate in full 'what thou tellst hath passed in heaven', Raphael reveals that he is not sure whether what

---

[70] Schultz, for instance (*op. cit.*, pp.1-2) gives us an interesting picture of the various anti-curiosity sermons that conservative Anglicans and Puritans undertook between 1600 and 1660. Interestingly, many of these 'didactic versifiers' quoted from the *mediaeval* divine, Bernard, 'to admonish those sinners who forgot that the Incarnation had been revealed to shepherds first, or who tried to plumb the depth of mysteries with wisdom's short line'. (See my Introduction, p.8.)

he is about to describe is 'lawful' or not.[71] It is little wonder then that the alert Adam should take full advantage of his mentor's vagueness to satisfy his own curiosity:

> But since thou hast vouchsafed
> Gently for our instruction to impart
> Things above earthly thought, which yet concerned
> Our knowing, as to highest wisdom seemed,
> Deign to descend now lower, and relate
> How first began this heaven which we behold
> Distant so high.[72] (VII, 80-87)

Troubled by doubts, Raphael can justify his rather bold initiatives as a narrator only by hoping to make Adam happier, though I think he does exaggerate his duties somewhat when he says:

> Yet what thou canst attain, which best may serve
> To glorify the maker, and infer
> Thee also happier, shall not be withheld
> Thy hearing, such commission from above
> I have received, to answer thy desire
> Of knowledge within bounds. (VII, 115-20)

If God directed him to make Adam happier, it was a very implicit direction indeed! However, it must also be admitted that Raphael does succeed in skilfully reconciling almost all his revelations (all except one in fact, as we shall see) to the benefit of Adam and his wife. Thus, although he begins the account of the fall of Satan,

---

[71] See V, 544-570.

[72] *Op. cit.*, p.361.

suspicious of its legality, he ends by showing that there is a definite moral to be gained by his listener from it (11 893-913).

When Adam gradually approaches the topic of natural science in Bk. VII however, Raphael becomes more alarmed and for the first time warns Adam against curiosity:

> Beyond abstain
> To ask, nor let thine own inventions hope
> Things not revealed, which the invisible king,
> Only omniscient, hath suppressed in night,
> To none communicable in earth or heaven:
> Enough is left besides to search and know. (VII, 120-125)

This warning is significant since it is in fact a presentation in miniature of the attitudes involved in the dialogue on astronomy. Knowledge, Raphael says, is not to be sought beyond the bounds of things revealed. For those things not revealed are not only shrouded in darkness but also unknowable. Here, as Fowler has suggested, it is possible that Milton makes a reference to scientific discoveries.[73] And the scepticism betrayed in this remark is to be further elaborated in the astronomical dialogue. The consolatory provision of intellectual inquiry which Raphael allows Adam is I think a typical example of the contradictions involved in Milton's dependence on the Scriptures for intellectual as well as spiritual guidance. Having announced that Revelation is all we need concern ourselves with, Milton attempts to avoid seeming an obscurantist by recommending a search after knowledge 'in measure'. This cannot but strike us as a

---

[73] See Milton, *op. cit.*, p.364, 1.121n.

most unconvincing intellectual consolation. An insistence on temperance and moderation may be a general Renaissance, even Baconian, quality. But if we are to equate (as we no doubt should, following the logic of the passage) the things we may explore to the things revealed, I fail to see what there is really left (let alone 'enough') to 'search and know' in things already explained. That all human knowledge (even after the Fall) is to be of this strange revelatory kind is seen in Raphael's closing words at the end of Book VII, where he states that his revelations have been made so that 'posterity informed by thee might know' (11 639-640). In other words Adam's progeny is to depend for its intellectual satisfaction solely on Adam's revelations, just as Adam himself must now depend on Raphael's. Raphael's speech thus blends religious truth and secularie truth (we saw a slighter instance of this in *Areopagitica*) in an unhappy mixture that tantalises the intellect with the prospect of free inquiry at the same time as it sets up moral-scriptural limitations for the unwary enthusiast whose natural curiosity it saw no wrong in exciting in the first place.

∼

The beginning of Book VIII confirms the authority of Revelation even more emphatically.[74] Adam prefixes his question on astronomical motions with strong assertions of his belief in Raphael's exceptional merit as a narrator.

---

[74] Incidentally, G. McColley ('Milton's Dialogue on Astronomy' in *PMLA*, 521, 1937, p.757) is, perhaps, the only critic who has pointed out that Milton intended to defend the seriptures in this dialogue. He suggests, though, that this scriptural defence is a *secondary* purpose of the dialogue, the primary one being the 'rebuke of cosmological speculation'. I myself believe that the two motives are really complementary and so equal in influence.

What Raphael has so far related to him are 'else by me unsearchable' and the doubt that still lingers in his mind 'only thy solution can resolve'. It is important to note here that the manner of Adam's reasoning is not really anti-Baconian (as most critics have deduced from his interest in final causes[75]) for he in fact draws his conclusions from his own observations of the physical world:

> When I behold this goodly frame, this world
> Of heaven and earth consisting, and compute
> Their magnitudes, this earth a spot, a grain,
> An atom, with the firmament compared
> And all her numbered stars, that seem to roll
> Spaces incomprehensible (for such
> Their distance argues and their swift return
> Diurnal) merely to officiate light
> Round this opacous earth, this punctual spot,
> One day and night; in all their vast survey
> Useless besides, reasoning I oft admire,
> How nature wise and frugal could commit
> Such disproportions. (VIII, 3.15-27)

Also, the negative replies of Raphael have been too easily attributed by scholars like Burden and Schultz, to what they consider the dangerousness of Adam's motives in posing his question.[76] Actually, Adam begins his query by calling the universe 'this goodly frame' and at the end of it he solemnly enters 'on studious thoughts abstruse' without the slightest indication of wanting to start a quarrel with his teacher. Both of these actions I think show that Adam is genuinely concerned about the problem he has encountered

---

[75] For example, see Schultz *op. cit. passim*.

[76] See Burden, *The Logical Epic*, p.116 and Schultz, *op. cit.*, p.182.

and that he has little intention of criticising the creation, which he has already recognized as a good thing. (The only phrases that could be taken to imply criticism are 'such disproportions' and 'superfluous hand' and both these are, in the context of Adam's scientific discussion, really quite technical and innocuous). In fact Milton himself absolves him of any 'unspoken cavils' (Schultz) when he makes Raphael comment: 'To ask or search I blame thee not' (1 66).

Before coming to Raphael's answer, let us pause for a moment to consider the little shuffle in the domestic scene that occurs at this point, with Eve leaving her husband and the angel to go 'forth among her fruits and flowers' (1 44). Eve, Milton is careful to explain, does not leave because she is incapable of comprehending 'what was high'. Rather, she chooses to have the discussion relayed to her later on by Adam when she is alone with him. The curious feature of her way of attending to intellectual problems is that she expects Adam 'to solve high dispute with conjugal caresses'. Eve's intellectual capacity has, we know, been impartially established. If then an intelligent being like her should regard the debate as so slight that it can be solved in the midst of lovemaking, is Milton suggesting through her that this is all the significance one need attach to this 'high dispute' about astronomy? Even if one explains Eve's peculiar evaluation of the argument to follow as being due to Milton's belief in the softer nature of women which demands a softer setting for the discussion, it is still significantly strange that Milton should so easily have allowed the astronomical dialogue to be trivialised into an incidental part of an amorous scene where Adam's 'words' have the same (if not less) importance as his 'caresses'.

With Eve out of the way, Raphael proceeds with his reply. Scientific inquiry is first generously pardoned, as though it would in fact, have been a sin if heaven were not 'as the Book of God before thee set wherein to read his wondrous works'! This again shows us the superiority that Milton clearly wants to grant the Scriptures even in scientific matters. It is this desire to establish scriptural supremacy that causes him to make the categorical dismissal of questions as to 'whether heaven move or earth' in 1 .70. Moreover, he recommends that Adam should learn the 'seasons, hours, or days, or months, or years' from the heavens. Milton's adoption of the utilitarian philosophy is thus seen to reappear in a new and narrow form in this dialogue. As for the unknown facts of astronomy, Raphael goes on to say,

> the rest
> From man or angel the great architect
> Did wisely to conceal. (V111, 70-72)

Why this action is wise we find out when Raphael explains that God's secrets are not 'revealed' because mankind ought to wonder ('admire') at them rather than study them minutely ('scan'). Raphael thus has gone so far as to say that it is better to gaze simply at all the unexplained facets of nature than to try to understand them.

What he next declares is even more alarmingly antiscientific. God, he says, will guard his secrets so firmly that man's conjectures will not only be futilely disputatious but also made the subject of God's laughter. This despicable picture of God laughing at man's intellectual endeavours includes an attack on scientific techniques and devices as well (11.79-84). As the particular terms Milton uses here are actually descriptions of methods employed by both

Copernican and Ptolemaic scientists[77] it is evident that Milton is contemptuous of all astronomical study in general. The cartoon pictures which Raphael evokes of astronomers when they come to model heaven and calculate the stars' may be an indictment especially of astronomical study as prescribed by the schoolmen (the term 'save the phenomena' as Fowler explains is a scholastic one), but in the absence of a qualifying commendation of newer astronomical methods I fail to see anything that positively redeems the anti-intellectualism of this passage. The next section of Raphael's speech is a rather surprising volte-face since in it he disregards his recent scorn of astronomy and attempts to justify (with his powers of logical 'reasoning' needless to say) the apparent anomaly remarked by Adam. The value of Raphael's arguments as a piece of Baconian thinking is, it must be noted, quite negligible. If experimental science based on physical observations is the quality of a good Baconian, then Raphael's speech falls far short of the standard. For, critical though he might be of Adam's teleological assumptions, what he himself recommends is not a closer observation of nature but a belief in the existence of final causes even though they may not be immediately apparent to Adam. The sun he says, shines for the benefit of thee earth's inhabitant', the heaven's 'wide circuit' is extraordinarily vast so that man may learn from it that 'he dwells not in his own' and the other 'partitions' of this universe are created for 'uses to his Lord best known'!

At the end of this explanation comes an almost cowardly afterword in which Raphael makes clear his non-committal attitude:

> But this I urge, Admitting motion in the heavens,
> to show Invalid that which thee to doubt it moved;
> Not that I so affirm, (VIII, 114-117)

---

[77] See Milton, *op.cit.*, p.400, 1.83 n.

There are, I think, two possible explanations for Raphael's unsatisfactory reply. One is that he just does not know what exactly is the truth about celestial motions and the other is that knowing it, he still will not tell. The first explanation is unlikely since it would make Raphael a rather stupid creature, for he has just flown through the heavens (see Bk. V, ll 247-274) and has had ample opportunity for observing various astronomical phenomena himself. The parenthetical, though so it seems to 'thee on earth' also shows that he, a sky-dweller, is exempt from such ignorance. Similarly, when he says later on that 'heaven is for thee too high to know what passes there' (ll 172-173), he obviously does not include himself in his comment. The second explanation then is the more probable one, in which case astronomical study is indeed an area of knowledge that is forbidden. However, the fact that Raphael hesitated even earlier on — before revealing details of the creation of the earth and the fall of the angels — afraid lest he should reveal forbidden knowledge shows that, though forbidden, astronomy is perhaps not *the* 'forbidden knowledge' of the Tree. Why then should it be so expressly forbidden when explanations of the other phenomena were allowed?

What Raphael himself says after his ambiguous 'Not that I so affirm' gives us a clue, I think:

> God to remove his ways from human sense,
> Placed heaven from earth so far, that earthly sight,
> If it presume, might err in things too high,
> And no advantage gain. (VIII, 119-122)

This is in effect the climax of all the anti-scientific tendencies that have gradually emerged in the course of the angel's conversation. If Milton's purpose in writing

Paradise Lost was to justify the ways of God to man, he stuck very faithfully indeed to that purpose. For what he is suggesting here in fact is that those things in nature that cannot be easily explained by the Scriptures (Raphael is clearly a scriptural commentator even though a very Miltonic one) are to be simply left alone! What is more appalling is that God has *deliberately* placed heaven from earth so far in order to confound the curious scientist and render his efforts useless.

This kind of justification of divine ways is quite unequivocally anti-intellectual. It does not even have the usual excuse of utilitarianism. For Raphael does not say that men will gain no advantage from studying the heavens but rather that God works in such a way that man may not gain any advantage from such study. As for the slighting references to the inadequacy of sense perception in these lines, I cannot doubt that even Bacon would have been somewhat horrified by them.[78]

Having described God's attitude towards human intellectual enterprise, Raphael then embarks on an impressive display of astronomical knowledge (Milton's habit of showing off his learning has apparently suffered little change from the days of the *Prolusions*) in order to strengthen his point about the folly of scientific inquiry vis-à-vis God's 'superior' wisdom. Here Raphael reveals that he is indeed aware (most probably even sure) that the sun is the centre of the universe and that the earth moves

---

[78] It is interesting to note that Schultz, in his account of the Baconian defense of naturalism (*op. cit.* p.38), states: 'If the captious should ask why God had hidden so much from us, Bacon replied with something like Milton's elaboration on Proverbs XXV: 2 — it was "as if according to the innocent play of children the divine Majesty took delight to hide his works, *to the end to have them found out*"' (my italics). This Baconian reply (see Bacon, *op. cit.*, p.58) is clearly at variance with Raphael's and Schultz is certainly wrong in associating Milton with Bacon on this point.

in 'three different motions' (the third motion, though an anachronistic Copernican belief, may still be valid in a prelapsarian world[79]). He even ventures so far as to believe that the moon and the other planets may be inhabited because they receive light from the earth just as it receives light from them (a syllogistic fallacy Milton drew from Kepler and Burton[80]).

The justification Raphael gives for all his conclusions is the familiar one of Miltonic utilitarianism. The sheer size of the planets suggests, in Milton's view, the existence of other inhabited worlds which adequately utilise nature's 'vast room':

> For such vast room in nature unpossessed
> By living soul, desert and desolate,
> Only to shine, yet scarce to contribute
> Each orb a glimpse of light, conveyed so far
> Down to this habitable, which returns
> Light back to them, is obvious to dispute. (VIII, 153-158)

Similarly, geocentricity appeals to his utilitarian reasoning in that it prevents so much waste of solar and planetary energy:

> What if the sun
> Be centre to the world, and other stars
> By his attractive virtue, and their own
> Incited, dance about him various rounds?
> Their wandering course now high, now low, then hid,

---

[79] See Milton, *op. cit.*, p.403, 1.130 n.

[80] See Milton, *op cit.*, p.404, 11.140-45 n.

> Progressive, retrograde, or standing still,
> In six thou seest, and what if seventh to these
> The planet earth, so steadfast though she seem,
> Insensibly three different motions move?
> Which else to several spheres thou must ascribe,
> Moved contrary with thwart obliquities,
> Or save the sun his labour, and that swift
> Nocturnal and diurnal rhomb supposed,
> Invisible else above all stars, the wheel
> If day and night; which needs not thy belief,
> Of earth industrious of her self fetch day
> Travelling east, and with her part averse
> From the sun's beam meet night, her other part
> Still luminous by his ray. (VIII, 122-40)

Having exhibited these careful arguments, Raphael goes on to discard them himself:

> But whether thus these things, or whether not,
> Whether the sun predominant in heaven
> Rise on the earth, or earth rise on the sun,
> He from the east his flaming road begin,
> Or she from west her silent course advance
> With inoffensive pace that spinning sleeps
> On her soft axle, while she paces even,
> And hears thee soft with the smooth air along,
> Solicit not thy thoughts with matters hid. (VIII, 159-67)

By this means he hopes to convince Adam that such astronomical theories, even utilitarian ones, are best avoided completely. Earlier (11.77-78) he had suggested that astronomy makes men the laughing stock of God. Now he supplies a reason for God's disdainful isolation from mankind. As heaven is anyway 'too high to know what passes there', Adam should clear his mind of astronomical thoughts and concentrate on what God expects of him:

> 'Leave them to God above, him serve and fear.' (VIII, 168).

Given the terrible cul-de-sac quality of Raphael's earlier portrayal of scientists 'left to their disputes' while 'God moves his laughter at their quaint opinions' on matters that have been deliberately 'hid', I cannot imagine what else there really is left for Adam to do except fear and serve such a God. But Raphael does give Adam some 'consolations':

> Joy thou
> In what he gives to thee, this Paradise
> And thy fair Eve. (VIII, 170-172)

The cosy happiness of Adam's present condition in Paradise (which Adam was not in doubt of anyway) then is the most that Raphael can offer as a satisfaction of Adam's intellectual thirst. Further contentment Adam is to draw from the fact that,

> thus far hath been revealed
> Not of earth only but of highest heaven. (VIII 177-178)

For, more than this does not 'concern thee and thy being'. Why this should be so is a moot question, in view of the fact that there is nothing more relevant or useful in Raphael's earlier information about the digestion of angels although Raphael finally justifies it by extracting an analogous lesson about the rewards of obedient living. (If Raphael saw fit, he could more easily have drawn a similar lesson from astronomical information. After all, as Adam remarks at the end of Raphael's 'angelic diet' speech, 'In contemplation of created things By steps we may ascend to God', V, 511-512). The answer to this question I think really stares at us in the face from out of Raphael's last injunction:

> Dream not of other worlds, what creatures there
> Live, in what state, condition or degree,
> Contented that thus far hath been revealed
> Not of earth only but of highest heaven. (VIII, 175-8)

The first part of this sentence states the prohibition and the second clearly explains it. Astronomy, Milton is saying, should be shunned because it seeks to know things that are not 'revealed'.

It is interesting to note that in spite of Raphael's largely negative attitude towards the intellect, the tone in which he delivers his justifications of God's ways is not indicative of an explicit anti-intellectualism. (He begins his answer by saying 'To ask or search I blame thee not') but rather suggests a brave defence of the anti-intellectualism of his master's methods.[81] But the tone of Adam's reply is quite different. Considering the sharpness of intellect revealed both in his questions and in the way in which he posed them, it does come as a bit of a shock that he should be so easily satisfied

---

[81] That this master is Milton himself as much as God is obvious, from the way Milton, rather than the God of Bk. V, manipulates Raphael's speech into so many extravagances.

with Raphael's half-answers and warnings and consolations. He is now 'cleared of doubt' and bursting with exaggerated praise of the angel:

> How fully hast thou satisfied me, pure
> Intelligence of heaven. (V111,180-181)

The curious lack of restraint in the tone of Adam's reaction is, I think, an effective psychological device designed to lend, by contrast, complete intellectual credibility to Raphael's more restrained and seemingly impartial answers. That Milton 'is playing the matter very cleverly' in this dialogue has already been suspected by Burden.[82] But he does not observe the particular intelligence of Milton's use of these contrasting tones. The man who began as an acute curious is now wholly converted to the teachings of Raphael. His extravagant mood makes him draw a series of new lessons which not only flatter God but also violently chastise his own intellectual enthusiasm. God, he exclaims, has been so kind as to 'bid dwell far off all anxious cares' in order that 'the sweet of life' may not be polluted. He himself feels guilty of 'wandering thoughts' and 'vain notions', though there was nothing 'unchecked' about the measured reasoning of his question. The final indictment of scientific curiosity[83] is made in a brutal manner, when Adam, in recognizing the 'prime wisdom' of knowing useful things, goes to the extreme of demolishing all astronomy (which, incidentally, is taken by all concerned in this dialogue to be quite incapable

---

[82] See Burden, *op. cit.*, p.120.

[83] A. Fowler thinks Adam is here referring to 'idle speculations of the intellect'. I doubt this entirely because the kind of 'frugal nature' speculation Adam employs is approved and even used by Raphael himself later on. (See Milton, *op. cit.*, p.407, ll.183-197 n).

of bringing benefit to mankind beyond the assistance it supplies in determining the hours and the seasons) as 'fume, or emptiness or fond impertinence' (VIII, 11.194-95). Thus what Raphael gracefully, but firmly, dismissed in his arguments, Adam now clumsily clouts into ignominy. It is almost as if Milton, in his anxiety to establish the justness of Raphael's defence of anti-intellectualism, thought it necessary to disgrace far-reaching scientific inquiry and in particular astronomy as an appropriate example of it, a little further by making Adam give it a horrible coup de grâce.[84]

The reasons for Milton's anti-intellectualism should be apparent by now.[85] The old obsession with the virtues of utilitarianism is now narrowed down to only 'that which lies before us in daily life'.[86] The youthful enthusiasm for boundless knowledge witnessed in the *Prolusions* and '*Of*

---

[84] That astronomy is an appropriate symbol, both Burden and Schultz (see Burden, *op. cit.*, p.118-119, & Schultz, *op. cit.* p.175) have convincingly proved. But they do not seem particularly disturbed by Milton's having dragged it and the intellectual endeavour it represents into this conversation when God himself made no mention of either of them while directing Raphael or even earlier, when setting the prohibition on the Tree of Knowledge.

[85] Grant McColley ('Milton's dialogue on Astronomy' *PMLA*, 52 i, pp. 757-762) suggests that Milton particularly attacked the Royal Society and one of its famous representatives, Wilkins, in this dialogue. This may quite probably have been the case though there is no definite proof for his theory.

[86] A. O. Lovejoy calls Hilton's pragmatism 'an obscurantist utilitarianism hostile to all disinterested intellectual curiosity and to all inquiry into unsolved problems about the physical world', ('Milton's Dialogue on Astronomy in *Reason and Imagination* ed. J. A. Mazzeo, N.Y. 1962, p.142). His further comment, though, that this extreme expression of pragmatism in no other book and at no other time could ... have been more incongruous, or unwittingly, more ironic' is rather misguided, as I intend to show in my next chapter.

Education' has now understandably faded, for it was never really an intellectual light, only an emotional glow fed by his anti-scholastic and anti-prelatic drives. He may have sincerely believed himself to have been a champion of Baconian science while writing those early works. But his worth as a genuine Baconian is here belied by the excesses that make him sharply criticise the intellect and the senses. These new excesses are clearly due to his strong (obligatory and willing) reliance on the Scriptures for authorisation of any area of human knowledge brought into discussion. Raphael is first permitted to give Adam all the knowledge that Milton can justify from the Scriptures. And then, in order to probe the sufficiency of scriptural revelation Milton goes to the extreme of denouncing, in a medieval scholastic fashion, all intellectual inquiry into things 'obscure and subtle' which do not find their raison d'être in the Scriptures.

CHAPTER 3
PARADISE LOST II

Apart from the long dialogue between Adam and Raphael, the other important intellectual 'problem' of *Paradise Lost* is Milton's treatment of the epic's central event — the Fall of Man at the Tree of Knowledge. Critical commentaries on this subject have ranged from Willey's discussion of a Psychological Fall and Lovejoy's account of a Fortunate Fall to Burden's analysis of it as though it were a long lesson in logic. All these discussions no doubt have their own validity as theories, but clearly as no more. So that, despite Mahood's description of one of them (Willey's) as 'irrefutable',[87] I think it would be advisable, when re-examining this aspect of Milton's epic for its intellectual implications, to free ourselves (not in order to assume a too aggressive approach, but to avoid a too easily sympathetic one) from all categorical conceptions of the Fall as Fortunate or Logical or Psychological. The first and only reference in the entire epic to God's actual commandment regarding the Tree (in the second person singular) is to be found in Adam's speech to Raphael in Book VIII:

> This Paradise I give thee, count it thine
> To till and keep, and of the fruit to eat;

---

[87] Mahood, *Poetry & Humanism*. (London, 1950), p.244.

> Of every tree that in the garden grows
> Eat freely with glad heart; fear here no death;
> But of the tree whose operation brings
> Knowledge of good and ill, which I have set
> The pledge of thy obedience and thy faith,
> Amid the garden by the tree of life,
> Remember what I wam thee, shun to taste,
> And shun the bitter consequence: for know,
> The day thou eat'st thereof, my sole command
> Transgressed, inevitably thou shalt die;
> From that day mortal, and this happy state
> Shalt loose, expelled from hence into a world
> Of woe and sorrow. (VIII, 11 319-33)

Here God describes the Tree as that 'whose operation brings knowledge of good and ill' and as that 'which I have set the pledge of thy obedience and thy faith'. (It is also described as being next to the Tree of Life, which both in Milton and in my discussion has no great significance). The prohibition on the tree is not to 'taste of it for by doing so Adam will incur death, a loss of his 'happy state', and an expulsion into a world of woe and sorrow'. This account of God's commandment differs from the original Biblical version (Genesis, 2, 17) in two of its details. The less remarkable of these two is the qualification of the penalty of death by the introduction of misery into the human condition. More important and relevant is the description of the Tree as 'a pleage of thy obedience and thy faith'. Milton's God has thus been careful to suggest that, apart from its virtue of providing knowledge of good and evil, it is what the poet earlier, in *De Doctrina Christiana*, called 'a kind of pledge or memorial of obedience'.[88]

---

[88] Milton, *Complete Prose Works*, ed. Wolfe and others, p.352.

Adam, in relating this 'rigid interdiction' to Eve (*Paradise Lost* IV, 11 419-30) describes it again in its dual character as 'a tree of knowledge' and 'the only sign of our obedience', though obviously stressing the latter quality more than the former. More interesting, however, is the way Milton makes Satan react to this speech, which he has overheard from his perch atop the Tree of Life. Satan is delighted that there is a divine Prohibition on the Tree of Knowledge of good and evil for it gives him a marvellous opportunity of destroying the happiness of his usurpers. The way in which he interprets this prohibition is especially significant. Unlike God and the innocent Adam, Satan places the utmost importance, not on the pledge of obedience, but on the knowledge hidden in this Tree. In fact, the proof of their obedience itself is, in his mind, their ignorance, and God's commands are consequently an 'envious' scheme to keep them low 'whom knowledge might exalt equal with gods'. It is thus on this particular 'desire to know' (and know all things, not merely good and evil) that Milton's Satan hopes to construct his evil plan. This, it will be immediately seen, is a subtle variation of the serpent's method in Genesis, where Eve is tempted with the promise of ethical knowledge alone (Genesis 3, 5).

Satan's first attempt at clouding man's innocence takes the form of a dream. In this dream, Satan enters Eve's unconscious mind and enacts with her the drama of the Fall up to the eating of the Forbidden Fruit. The manner in which he focuses Eve's attention and appetite onto the fruit is characteristic of the Miltonic Satan. In keeping with the Biblical account of the palatal attractions of the fruit (Genesis 3, 6) Satan charges his address to the 'fair plant' with luscious descriptions of the fruits sweetness:

> And O fair plant, said he, with fruit surcharged,
> Deigns none to ease thy load and taste thy sweet.
> (V, 58-59)

And:

> O fruit divine,
> Sweet of thy self, but much more sweet thus cropt.
> (V, 67-68)

But the major thrust of his arguments derives from the knowledge-giving virtues he attributes to the fruit:

> Is knowledge so despised?
> Or envy, or what reserve forbids to taste? (V, 60-61)

And:

> Forbidden here, it seems, as only fit
> For Gods, yet able to make gods of men. (V, 69-70)

This fruit is not only capable of lending man a divine awareness, but also of literally elevating him from the earthly level to the heights of heaven:

> Not to earth confined,
> But sometimes in the air, as we, sometimes
> Ascend to heaven. (V, 78-80)

The purpose of this new addition to the fruit's powers is to entice Eve 'to see what life the gods live there'. This preparatory dream-temptation, thus, already gives us a hint of the ulterior motives that inform Milton's portrayal of Satan the Seducer. Satan is made to fervently praise the pursuit of knowledge and to ally this curiosity to a desire to probe into the ways of God. This plan of Satan's will with no difficulty be recognized as the 'evil' counterpart of Raphael's astronomical speech in Book VIII with its clear injunctions to leave God's ways alone:[89]

> God to remove his ways from human sense,
> Placed heaven from earth so far, that earthly sight,
> If it presume, might err in things too high,
> And no advantage gain. (VIII, 119-122)

And:

> Solicit not thy thoughts with matters hid,
> Leave them to God above. (VIII, 167-168)

In fact, the more convincing Milton makes Satan appear in his temptation-speeches the more powerful will be Milton's own ultimate refutations of these Satanic arguments.

The dream effects of eating the fruit (which Eve understandably offers little resistance to) are similar to the real effects which she and her husband will soon experience. She first finds herself exalted 'up to the clouds' and is then suddenly dropped down into what she imagines is sleep but is, in fact, death. Her fear and hatred of this dream however reveal that she is yet sinless and Adam therefore kindly absolves her of all blame:

---

[89] Satan even informs Eve, like Raphael (VII, 11 115-117), that his intention is to make her 'happier':
'happy thou art
Happier thou mayet be' (V, 11 75-76).

> Evil into the mind of God or man
> May come and go, so unapproved, and leave
> No spot or blame behind: which gives me hope
> That what in sleep thou didst abhor to dream
> Waking thou never wilt consent to do. (V, 117-121)

The Satanic complaint that provides a preamble to the actual Fall is to be noted for its emphatically anthropocentric remarks:

> As God in heaven
> Is centre, yet extends to all, so thou
> Centring receivest from all those orbs; in thee,
> Not in themselves, all their known virtue appears
> Productive in herb, plant, and nobler birth
> Of creature animate with gradual life
> Of growth, sense, reason, all summed up in man.
> (IX, 107-114)

Devoid as this speech is of the obligatory praise of the Creator which Raphael insisted on in the contemplation of any of God's works, it is indicative, as Fowler (see, Milton, *Paradise Lost*, edited by Fowler, p.444, 11.103-113n) suggests, of Milton's criticism of humanism per se. We already see here that the largely anthropocentric vision of life which inspired the rhetoric of the *Prolusions* has been somewhat reduced to fit his now uncompromisingly theocentric philosophy.

The conversation that follows between Adam and Eve is a vital part of Milton's moral justification of the Fall. For in it Adam describes the delicate relationships between Will and Reason, and Reason and God. Although Will is 'free', it follows its superior, Reason. And although Reason is made 'erect', it can still go 'wrong' if it does not adhere to its master God, and instead does 'what god expressly hath forbid'. With this account of the working of the human mind, Milton both establishes the 'freedom' of man's condition when he broke the 'pledge of obedience' and gives us a reason for Adam's allowing Eve to leave his side despite his awareness of the dangers of such an action. In fact, as Fowler points out (see Milton, *op. cit.*, p.458 ll.370-5n), the separation of Eve from Adam is made to accentuate artistically the vulnerable relationship between the reason and the will:

> For thy stay, not free, absents thee more;
> Go in thy native innocence, rely
> On what thou hast of virtue, summon all,
> For God towards thee hath done his part, do thine.
> (IX, 372-375)

The poetic-dramatic passages that follow, of Eve's walk to the groves and Satan's subsequent espial and admiration of her innocent beauty lead us directly to the fatal temptation. The seduction of Eve is, as I hinted earlier, a powerful elaboration of the shadowy scenes of evil that crossed Eve's mind in Book V. As in her dream, the figure of her tempter itself assumes an almost voluptuous fascination. Only, the 'dewy locks' of her imagined tormentor have now given place to a serpentine 'turret crest' and 'sleek enamelled neck'. This sensual aspect of the temptation Milton borrowed not from the Bible but from literary tradition, contemporary and classical (see Milton, op. cit., p. 468, 11.496-504n) and as such, it has more to say about the poetic (and perhaps moral) colouring of Milton's account of the Fall than about its intellectual character.

Satan's address to Eve, though, is a clever appeal, through her senses, to her mind. Her beauty is described by him in the most lofty terms: 'the heaven of mildness', 'thy awful brow', 'fairest resemblance of thy maker fair' — and then immediately contrasted with their plain, even savage, surroundings:

> But here
> In this enclosure wild, these beasts among,
> Beholders rude, and shallow to discern
> Half what in thee is fair, one man except,
> Who sees thee? (IX, 542-546)

So that, logically as well as artistically, Satan arrives at the conclusion that she 'shouldnt be seen a Goddess among Gods'. This is a prelude to his larger technique of making her strive for equality with God. Eve is immediately struck by the serpent's use of human language and his human sense. And this gives Satan a good opportunity to describe the Forbidden Fruit in as tantalising a fashion as he can. The very first quality he focuses her attention on is the accession of rationality. Wholly ignoring the original qualifications of the Tree's knowledge as 'knowledge of good and evil', he constructs his eulogy of the Tree on a distinction between 'abject thoughts low' and things 'high':

> I was at first as other beasts that graze
> The trodden herb, of abject thoughts and low,
> As was my food, nor aught but food discerned
> Or sex, and apprehended nothing high. (IX, 571-574)

Of course he was originally drawn to the 'fair apples' by their savoury attractions, it being, as mentioned earlier, a biblical necessity to invest the Tree with physical charm:[90]

> I nearer drew to gaze;
> When from the boughs a savoury odour blown,
> Grateful to appetite, more pleased my sense
> Than smell of sweetest fennel or the teats
> Of ewe or goat dropping with milk at even,
> Unsucked of lamb or kid, that tend their play.
> (IX,578-83)

The effects of the fruit on Satan, according to his inventions, are 'a degree of reason in my inward powers' and 'speech'. Significantly, the first use he puts his new found faculty of reasoning to is 'speculation high and deep'. For, we realize, Milton here wishes us to scorn Satan's intellectual enthusiasm as the unfavourable activity Raphael sternly checked in Adam not long before (VIII, 11.173-78). Satan's thoughts are especially (and 'perversely', Milton would no doubt have us think) directed towards 'heaven' and only then 'the earth' or 'middle'. Worse, this contemplation of the universe leads not to a glorification of its Creator but to an adoration of the human being:

> But all that fair and good in thy divine
> Semblance, and in thy beauty's heavenly ray
> United I beheld. (IX, 606-608)

---

[90] A lot has been made of the particular physical qualities of the Tree — see, for example, Burden's intricate description of the Tree changing its appearance at every stage of the logical development of Satan's, Eve's, and Adam's speeches in *The Logical Epic* (London 1967) pp.124-49 — but I do not think this has any significant relevance to our particular examination.

Again we observe that the feelings that now prompt Milton to give Satan such arguments are not only anti-intellectual but also rather anti-humanistic.

Eve then (strangely forgetful of her dream) allows herself to be led by the serpent to the Tree itself. On reaching it, however, she recognizes it as the Forbidden Tree and informs Satan of the interdiction that bars her from it. It is significant that even while resigning herself to abstinence she speaks fondly of the Fruit,

> Serpent, we might have spared our coming hither,
> Fruitless to me, though fruit be here to excess,
> The credit of whose virtue rest with thee,
> Wondrous indeed, if cause of such effects.
> But of this tree we may not taste nor touch; (IX, 647-51)

obviously longing to share its effects with Satan. Repeating God's instructions, it may also be remarked, she sticks to the original notion of the Tree as a symbol of obedience, and is afraid of death as the punishment of disobedience. Satan, though, is not in the least deterred by Eve's fear of the divine commandment and instead builds his own intelligent temptation on this fear. It is curious that the appearance of Satan as he delivers his fatal speech is described by Milton in terms of classical oration. Satan's oratorical attitudes may have been designed only as a parody of those of the Romans and the Greeks. But the very fact that Milton now finds it so easy to put classical eloquence to satanic use — indeed the effusive classical manner is seen to offer a contrast to the 'high power' of Raphael's mild speeches earlier on, and the almost genuine note of mockery in 'Stood in himself collected, while each part, Motion, each act won audience ere the tongue', already betray, I think, the growing lack of respect for the classics which will find its fullest expression in *Paradise Regained*.[91]

The content of this hymn to the Tree is of crucial importance. Concentrating once again on its knowledge-giving power, he apostrophizes the Tree as:

> O sacred, wise and wisdom-giving plant
> Mother of Science. (IX, 679-80)

The aspect he appreciates most in the knowledge offered by the Tree is that it enables him to determine the 'causes' of things and to freely analyse the wisdom of 'highest agents'. These consequences of 'science' are clearly what Milton feared most as threats to scriptural authority and the Christian Faith, and he no doubt thought it necessary to attack them here as part of the Satanic method. The actual account of the temptation in the Book of Genesis (3.5), it may be remembered, restricts Satan's praise of the Tree to the complete moral knowledge it can bestow on man. Satan's next strategic device is to quell Eve's fear of death:

> Queen of this universe, do not believe
> Those rigid threats of death; ye shall not die;
> How should ye? By the fruit? It gives you life
> To knowledge. By the threatener? Look on me,
> Me who have touched and tasted, yet both live,
> And life more perfect have attained than fate
> Meant me, by venturing higher than my lot. (IX, 684-90)

---

[91] See my next chapter.

Again, Satan does not simply declare that he continues to live in spite of the supposed penalty attached to the Fruit. Instead, he says that he has now achieved a life 'more perfect than fate meant me, by venturing higher than my lot'. This then is another 'evil' of knowledge and the thirst for knowledge. For man, when inspired by this desire, may aspire higher than is permitted by the 'lot' imposed on him by 'Fate' or 'God'.

When in the next section of his argument, Satan brings in God himself in support of his seduction, he properly refers to the Tree's knowledge as the 'knowledge of good and evil'. Here, as in the dream, he also implies that a desire to make man 'happier' is one of his motives (just as it was Raphael's before him). The very convincing arguments that he puts forth to prove that knowledge of good and evil will in fact lead to a happy state,

> Achieving what might lead
> To happier life, knowledge of good and evil;
> Of good, how just? Of evil, if what is evil
> Be real, why not known, since easier shunned?
> (IX, 696-99)

have prompted critics like Willey to conclude that Milton meant the Fall to represent a necessary stage in the intellectual evolution of men.[92] This deduction may be valid to a certain extent, especially since Milton employs similar arguments relating to the post-lapsarian benefits of knowledge and right reason in *Areopagitica*. But it must nonetheless be noted that the knowledge Milton

---

[92] 'Lovejoy's thesis of the Fortunate Fall sensibly restricts itself to the theological benefits of the Fall of Man. See Lovejoy, 'Milton and the Paradox of the Fortimate Fall", *ELH*, 4, 1937, pp.161-79.

is discussing here (and in the other passages quoted by Willey in *The Seventeenth Century Background*, London, 1934 pp.255-56, for example) is not all knowledge but knowledge of good and evil, an important moral qualification which quite belies the second deduction that Willey goes on to make about Milton's Renaissance humanism:

> Milton was a Promethean, a Renaissance humanist in the toils of a myth of quite contrary import, a myth which yearned as no Milton could, for the blank innocence and effortlessness of a golden age. (Willey, op. cit., p.255)

The major force of Willey's argument, it will be seen, derives from the sharp distinction he makes between the biblical myth and Milton's poetic transformations- a distinction that is essentially false since the mythical Tree itself does not hide all knowledge and intellectual endeavour (the opposite of 'blank ignorance and effortlessness'), but a mere ethical awareness of life's realities, and Milton's Tree too is really of this kind except in the Satanic context.

The manner in which Milton makes Satan proceed with his argument is indeed most intelligent. For Satan both adheres to the biblical myth and at the same time, reverts, by implication, to his original suggestion that the Tree possesses a full, 'Promethean', knowledge which will liberate man from both ignorance and lowliness:

> Why but to keep ye low and ignorant,
> His worshippers; he knows that in the day
> Ye eat thereof, your eyes that seem so clear,
> Yet are but dim, shall perfectly be then

> Opened and cleared, and ye shall be as gods,
> Knowing both good and evil as they know.
> That ye should be as gods, since I as man,
> Internal man, is but proportion meet,
> I of brute human, ye of human gods. (IX, 704-12)

The claims of divine power that he makes for the knowledge obtainable from the Tree are strengthened by his next suggestion that it is really quite easy to attain godhead since the gods themselves, or at least the gods that forbid knowledge (Satan here argues from a dualistic viewpoint) cannot be extraordinarily superior beings:

> And what are gods that man may not become
> As they, participating godlike food?
> The gods are first, and that advantage use
> On our belief, that all from them proceeds;
> I question it, for this fair earth I see,
> Warmed by the sun, producing every kind,
> Them nothing: if they all things, who enclosed
> Knowledge of good and evil in this tree,
> That whoso eats thereof, forthwith attains
> Wisdom without their leave? (IX, 716-25)

Satan then concludes with his classic question 'And wherein lies the offence that man should thus attain to know?' adding, in answer, that God just cannot forbid knowledge since envy (the only reason for such a prohibition) cannot 'dwell in heavenly breasts'.

The effect of this speech on Eve is, as in her dream, quite immediately successful. His 'persuasive words' are 'impregned with reason, to her seeming, and with truth' (Milton herein indicates that he himself does not believe any of Satan's arguments). The physical attractions of the fruit itself, combined with her natural appetite at noon, complete the perfection of Satan's well-planned seduction. Before eating of the fruit, though, Eve recites to herself a justification of her intended act. In this quiet musing (which is for the most part a repetition of Satan's points), it is interesting to note that Milton makes her refer to the Tree with splendid ambiguity as 'the Tree of knowledge, knowledge both of good and evil' when in fact God called it quite plainly 'the tree of knowledge of good and evil'. The slant in her silent speech however seems to be towards the purely 'intellectual' aspect of the fruit, for she calls it 'intellectual food', 'of virtue to make wise', and is evidently attracted most by the reasoning and discerning power it has endowed the erstwhile 'irrational' serpent with:

> He hath eaten and lives,
> And knows, and speaks, and reasons and discerns
> Irrational till then. (IX, 764-66)

While eating the fruit, Milton tells us, Eve is absorbed by its extraordinarily delicious 'taste', but he adds that this is perhaps on account of her 'expectation high of knowledge' and her hopes of 'godhead' clearly indicating to us that these are her most sinful motives (Willey's description of the Psychological Fall as the 'result of disobedience, not of knowledge', is surely inadequate in the light of these lines).

Having eaten of it, her immediate physical reaction is that of 'jocund and boon' inebriation, in which flushed mood she vows to tend the tree of operation 'blest to sapience' each morning. The reason for this extreme solicitude on behalf of the tree is, again, that she may thus 'grow mature in knowledge as the gods who all things know'. (Interestingly she also makes a distinction like Satan between two sets of gods, showing that she is, in effect, a satanic spokesman now). Her thanksgiving speech also includes 'experience' as the 'best guide' for, through it, she believes she has attained wisdom. If Milton intended here — as he very probably did to attack experience, as opposed to obedience, since it lead to illusory power, the force of such a criticism cannot but be slight, as the evidence he gives us for it the story of Eve and Adam's Fall is only contextually, and not generally, valid. Another strange feature of the apple's effect on Eve as described by Milton (a feature he drew from older sources, as Fowler points out[93]) is that it is capable of disturbing the traditional relationship between man and women (IX, 817-26). Knowing as we do Milton's 'Turkish' views on women and women's education, the crafty intellectual enthusiasm Eve exhibits here must surely have been meant to represent a strong argument against all indiscriminate knowledge-giving sources! Eve's fear of death, though, has not left her, and this presents her with a reason to share her 'bliss or woe' with Adam. Before leaving the Tree, she humbly bows to 'the power that dwelt within it' — a blasphemous adoration (she now worships Knowledge as she once worshipped God) which Milton evidently considered one of the most hateful dangers of the 'sciential sap'.

Eve's temptation of Adam is marked, once again, by its insistence on the 'godly' quality of her recent elation. The tree, she reveals, is 'of divine effect. To open eyes and make them gods who taste'. She quotes with enthusiasm the example of Satan's evolution into a sensible creature:

> The serpent wise,
> Or not restrained as we, or not obeying,
> Hath eaten of the fruit, and is become,
> Not dead, as we are threatened, but thenceforth

---

[93] See Milton, *op. cit.*, p.486, 1.821-3n

> Endued with human voice and human sense,
> Reasoning to admiration, (IX, 867-72)

The effects the fruit has had on herself are described as being proportionately divine:

> I
> Have also tasted, and have also found
> The effects to correspond, opener mine eyes,
> Dim erst, dilated spirits, ampler heart,
> And growing up to godhead; (IX, 873-77)

We cannot know exactly how much of Eve's account is sincere and how much deceptive because Milton has not told us in any explicit form what the precise effect of the fruit on Eve has been. That she has actually been thrown into an extraordinary ebullience by it is plain enough from her strange adoration of the Tree. That this effusiveness is partly due to her hopes of godhead is also evident. But the vital question of the kind of knowledge she has attained or thinks she has attained is left ambiguously unanswered. Yet the total absence of praise (real or feigned) for any newfound ethical discrimination indicates again that the knowledge she now venerates is all knowledge, godlike knowledge. We see thus that in working out Satan's temptation of Eve, her Fall and her seduction of Adam, Milton consistently and purposely develops an extra-scriptural, accusatory, bias towards the sin of knowledge for knowledge's sake, in order to discredit extreme intellectual ardour.[94] Incidentally, the Bible at this juncture is totally mute [Genesis, 3, 6] though, unlike Milton's clever use of it, it offers no ambiguity at all since there is

---

[94] Here we may compare Hilton's treatment of the Fall with Bacon's, as I hinted in my Introduction (see my Introduction, p.10n.)

nowhere any doubt that the knowledge of the Tree is the knowledge of good and evil.

Eve intensifies the potency of her temptation by adding to the enticements of knowledge, the shared joys of love:

> For bliss, as thou hast part, to me is bliss,
> Tedious, unshared with thee, and odious soon.
> Thou therefore also taste, that equal lot
> May join us, equal joy, as equal love; (IX, 879-82)

And it is interesting that it is this latter aspect that really convinces Adam of the need to follow his wife into damnation. That they are damned he is in no doubt of. For most probably on account of Raphael's warnings and his own 'higher intellectual', he has a superior awareness of the whole situation:[95]

> How art thou lost, how on a sudden lost,
> Defaced, deflowered, and now to death devote?
> Rather how hast thou yielded to transgress
> The strict forbiddance, (IX, 900-904)

(It is significant also that in his own criticism of Eve [ll.921-25] he calls her 'adventurous' — a term that one immediately relates to the 'experience' Eve sinfully worshipped in the Tree). But his fear of parting from his beloved wife makes him quickly decide to share her fate with her. Having made this decision, he attempts to justify his imminent Fall by rationalizing it (ll.926-51). One feature of this rationalization is particularly interesting. While recognizing the inevitability of a divine punishment

---

[95] This is, of course, in keeping with the Biblical judgement of Adam. See for e.g., I Tim., 2, 14.

of some sort, he nevertheless hopes that they may still ascend to godhead. Thus, although the principal sin of Milton's Adam is what in *De Doctrina Christiana* is called the sin of 'excessive luxuriousness', yet it is also laced; as Fowler suggests (see Milton, *op. cit.*, p.493, 1.936n), with the sin of knowledge which informed his wife's fall. Eve's rhapsodic commendation of Adam's decision (11.961-89) dwells chiefly on his brave proof of love, but again also insists on the possibility of their attaining a 'life augmented, opened eyes, new hopes, new joys'.

The eating of the fruit by Adam is in Milton's view of the Scriptures (*De Doctrina Christiana* Bk. I, Ch. XI) the moment at which Man's original sin first comes into being for it is then that 'carnal desire' is first aroused. The proceedings which went before this constitute what he calls 'actual sin' 'committed not only through actions as such but also through words and thoughts'.[96] And the 'thoughts and words' that Milton wished to charge his Adam and Eve with are, as we have seen, primarily (though perhaps not only, as the comprehensive list of sins in *De Doctrina Christiana* Bk.I, Ch.XI seems to indicate) those that aim at attaining a full, godlike, knowledge that may displace the proper authority and venerability of their creator.

The erotic scene that results from Adam's completion of the original mortal sin is soon followed by a more strictly Biblical account of the opening of their eyes. Having begun his Fall as a test of obedience, and then developed it through knowledge-orientated temptations (more so in the case of

---

[96] It is important to note that in *De Doctrina Christiana* Bk. I, Ch. XI Milton actually absolves Adam and Eve of any deliberate desire to provoke God's anger — a concession which must rob the Psychological Fall theory of much of its strength. In fact Milton classifies the loss of 'right reason' (which engenders the wrong motives of a Psychological Fall) under the 'penalty of sin' rather than under 'actual sin' itself. This is reflected in *Paradise Lost*, ll.1125-1131 too.

Eve than in the case of Adam), Milton here finally manages to reconcile it to the Book of Genesis. The knowledge that the fallen pair obtain -

> up they rose
> As from unrest, and each other viewing,
> Soon found their eyes how opened, and their minds
> How darkened; innocence that as a veil
> Had shadowed them from knowing ill, was gone,
> (IX, 1051-1055)

and

> since our eyes
> Opened we find indeed and find we know
> Both good and evil, good lost, and evil got, (IX, 1070-72)

- is ultimately seen to be the knowledge of good and evil promised and described in the Bible (Genesis 3,5-7,22). This knowledge, as in the Bible (Genesis 3, 7, 16-19), initially revolves around their new sexual self-consciousness and is then followed by other penalties such as 'high passions, anger, hate, mistrust, suspicion, and discord.'

~

The intellectual and moral corrective to the entire episode of the Fall of Man is provided by the series of visions and narrations that Michael offers Adam in Books XI and XII. Michael's task, as outlined by God, is entirely prophetic and consolatory,

> If patiently thy bidding they obey,
> Dismiss them not disconsolate; reveal
> To Adam what shall come in future days, (XI, 112-14)

In Michael's own words, however, this task is enlarged (it being apparently an angelic quality to outdo their master's expectations) to include a set of moral lessons on 'safe' living:

> know I am sent
> To shew thee what shall come in future days
> To thee and to thy offspring; good with bad
> Expect to hear, supernal grace contending
> With sinfulness of men; thereby to learn
> True patience, and to temper joy with fear
> And pious sorrow, equally inured
> By moderation either state to bear,
> Prosperous or adverse: so shalt thou lead
> Safest thy life, and best prepared endure
> Thy mortal passage when it comes. (XI, 1.356-66)

That Michael is meant to represent a holy counterpart to Satan is clear when Adam gratefully calls him 'safe guide', obviously remembering the other dangerous guide who recently visited his wife. Besides, the visions that Michael is to 'open' Adam's eyes to are to be regarded as the true opening of eyes in opposition to the intellectual awakening desired by both Eve and Adam at the Tree of Knowledge. This is clearly suggested by Michael's careful pushing of Adam's eyes in order to get rid of the obscuring effects of 'that false fruit that promised clearer sight' (1.413).

In the course of Michael's narration, it is important to observe that Adam once interrupts to exclaim:

> O sent from heaven,
> Enlightener of my darkness, gracious things
> Thou hast revealed, those chiefly which concern
> Just Abraham and his seed: now first I find
> Mine eyes true opening, and my heart much eased,
> Erewhile perplexed with thoughts what would become
> Of me and all mankind; but now I see
> His day, in whom all nations shall be blest,
> Favour unmerited by me, who sought
> Forbidden knowledge by forbidden means. (XII, 270-79)

Of the two important features of this ejaculation, one is that Adam now accepts fully what Raphael persistently hinted at earlier on, namely that his eyes' true opening is the 'gracious things thou hast revealed'. And as both Raphael's and Michael's revelations are scriptural ones we are left in little doubt of the particular nature of the weapon with which Milton thwarts all Satanic intellectual advances in *Paradise Lost*. The second, equally arresting, feature is that Adam defines his chief failing as his having sought 'forbidden knowledge by forbidden means'. The forbidden knowledge in this context inevitably and tellingly points to those kinds of knowledge not included in the instructions given by Adam's 'Enlightener of ... darkness'. (Incidentally the 'forbidden means' too seems to refer to the mere plucking of the forbidden fruit and scarcely hints at any pre-lapsarian psychological defects!)

At the end of Michael's speech, Adam (as at the conclusion of Raphael's astronomical discourse) declares:

> How soon hath thy prediction, seer blest,
> Measured this transient world, the race of time,
> Till time stand fixed: beyond is all abyss,
> Eternity, whose end no eye can reach.
> Greatly instructed I shall hence depart,
> Greatly in peace of thought, and have my fill
> Of knowledge, what this vessel can contain;
> Beyond which was my folly to aspire. (XII, 553-60)

This is indeed the final touch to the stunted intellectualism of *Paradise Lost*. What Michael has 'measured' in his scriptural visions and narrations is the ultimate intellectual food Adam can hope to have. The rest is 'all abyss, Eternity whose end no eye can reach'. Besides, these revelations of Michael's are all supposed to have a utilitarian value ('What this vessel can contain').[97] The rest 'was my folly to aspire' — again indicating that he (and Eve of course) aspired after knowledge per se (generally equated with futile knowledge) rather than the knowledge of good and evil.

On hearing this from his pupil, Michael is naturally overjoyed and so bestows his benediction on him:

> This having learned, thou hast attained the sum
> Of wisdom; hope no higher, though all the stars
> Thou knew'st by name, and all the ethereal powers,
> All secrets of the deep, all nature's works,
> Or works of God in heaven, air, earth, or sea, (XII, 575-79)

---

[97] See Samuel *op. cit.*, for examples of assimilable and unassimilable intellectual food in Milton's works.

This reference to 'secrets of the deep' brings to our mind the speech of Uriel and Satan in Book III where he commends Satan's desire to 'witness' (synonymous with the 'admire' of Raphael's speech later on) God's works, but warns him of the impossibility of finding out their causes since they have been hid deep (heralding Raphael's 'God to remove his ways from human sense / Placed heaven from earth so far, that earthly sight / If it presume, might err in things too high / And no advantage gain'). The intellectual merit of Michael's tutorship is thus of a kind with those of his fellow-angels. And that all these lectures are meant to be violently contrasted with the intellectual method of Satan in the garden of Eden is one of the major thematic interests of Milton's epic. I have already indicated at several points in my discussion of *Paradise Lost*, what such a treatment of the original scriptural material tells us of Milton's own opinions of the intellect, and, more particularly, the intellect in relation to the Scriptures. There only remains to be highlighted the last dreams that Eve has in Eden, under the influence of Michael. These 'gentle dreams' are obviously designed as an angelic balm for the 'evil' effects of the first Satanic dream in Book V:

> Her also I with gentle dreams have calmed
> Portending good, and all her spirits composed
> To meek submission: (XII, 595-97)

Whereas Satan gave her, at least a few moments of 'high exaltation' on the wings of knowledge, all Michael will allow himself to offer her is 'portents of good' (all scriptural no doubt) that efficiently lull her into a 'meek submission'!

CHAPTER 4
PARADISE REGAINED

The temptation of knowledge in Milton's last poetic work *Paradise Regained* - though *Samson Agonistes* and *Paradise Regained* were published together in 1671, it has now been convincingly demonstrated by scholars like W.R. Parker and J. Carey that *Samson Agonistes* was almost certainly composed earlier than *Paradise Regained*[98] - offers us the culmination of his increasingly anti-intellectual attitudes and clearly points to the scriptural basis of these attitudes. The invocation which opens this brief epic announces the theme of obedience as the poem's principal motif:

> I who erewhile the happy garden sung,
> By one man's disobedience lost, now sing
> Recovered Paradise to all mankind,
> By one man's firm obedience fully tried (I, 1-4)

We immediately realize that all the temptations of *Paradise Regained* are meant to be considered as temptations of obedience just as the temptations of Adam and Eve in *Paradise Lost* were. But whether Milton adheres closely to

---

[98] See Carey in *Milton, Complete Shorter Poems*, edited by Carey (Koyman, 1971) p.328.

this ostensible purpose or whether, as in *Paradise Lost*, he weaves into the temptations his own personal intellectual attitudes is still to be seen.

God, when predicting the temptations says:

> He now shall know I can produce a man
> Of female seed, far abler to resist
> All his solicitations, and at length
> All his vast force, and drive him back to hell,
> (1,150-53)

This sounds like an expression of pique against the claims made by Satan in *Paradise Lost* (IV, 1.111) that he will succeed in holding 'Divided empire with heaven's king, and against the Satanic doubts entertained by his first human creation' in IX, 11.947-50. We already realize here that not only is Milton's Satan an extraordinarily potent adversary but that his God's powers too are in considerable need of confirmation and congratulation. It is this very real sense of danger inherent in God's words that I think gives the impending temptation of knowledge most of its piquancy.

The temptation of Athens, which Milton introduced without a scriptural warrant into his loose interpretation of the Gospel according to St. Luke, is the temptation that has the closest connection with that of Eve and Adam in *Paradise Lost*. For, as we have already seen in my last chapter, Milton's Edenic pair fell largely through their desire for knowledge, a desire which was, as I have shown, an equally non-scriptural invention. If, as Schultz has done, we divide Satan's strategy into 'Fraudulent deceptions', 'snares' and 'terrors' (a division based on the predictions in I, 11. 97,179) then we realize that the '*vita contemplativa*' is indeed the last of Satan's snares and therefore clearly designed to be the most dangerous.[99] (The 'terrors' of future suffering and of physical violence that follow are nowhere as formidable as the two major snares of the '*vita activa*' and the '*vita contemplativa*'.)

Before we consider the actual temptation it would be advisable to recollect what Christ has already said about knowledge and truth in the earlier Books. Christ's first words are a meditation on the relative values of his various actions up to that point (ll.196ff). And significantly I think much of Christ's musings resembles Milton's own life story. When he was yet a child, he says he set his mind wholly 'to learn and to know' and 'thence do public good'. For he believed that his great destiny was 'to promote all truth, all righteous things'. The means he employed to achieve this end reveal that, not unlike Milton, he always had a religious view of 'truth'. He first perused the Law of God and then aspired to victorious deeds that would 'rescue Israel from the Roman yoke' (just as Milton himself did during the Puritan-Royalist battles). Finally, however, he decided that it was more heavenly to 'conquer willing hearts', 'teach the erring soul' and 'subdue' the stubborn — a decision that was most fervently commended by his mother (ll.229-232).[100] Bearing the comparison between Christ's life and Milton's still in mind, we realize that the subordination of the earlier reading to the later task of preaching the word of God must indeed be a reflection of the need Milton himself now feels to concentrate singly on his Christian purposes as being far more heavenly than his youthful attempts to 'learn and know' and to act heroically.

---

[99] See Schultz, *op. cit.*, p.225.

[100] 'These growing thoughts' (l.227) do not merely refer to Christ's new notions but also suggests that these notions are indicative of a spiritual *growth* in Christ. .

When Christ is bidden to the wilderness as the first stage of his entry into the world and its ministry, he remarks,

> And now by some strong motion I am led
> Into this wilderness, to what intent
> I learn not yet, perhaps I need not know;
> For what concerns my knowledge God reveals.
> (I, 290-93)

echoing so many of the themes of *Paradise Lost*. He obeys his father's instructions submissively and questions nothing. For what he 'does not know' is, according to the rules of Christian logic, what he 'need not know': what he needs to know will be 'revealed'. Having reached the wilderness Christ soon encounters his antagonist and the temptations begin directly. During the early combats it is interesting to note that one of the characteristics of Satan that Christ sharply criticizes is his habit of directing men's 'future life' through oracles, portents and dreams (I, ll.405-64). This, as Carey points out[101] is based on the patristic view that the shrines of pagan oracles were often occupied by fallen angels. But the way in which Milton develops this notion is especially significant. Christ's attack on Satan's oracular faculty begins with a description of the invalidity of oracular truth:

> Yet thou pretend'st to truth; all oracles
> By thee are given, and what confessed more true
> Among the nations? that hath been thy craft,
> By mixing somewhat true to vent more lies.
> But what have been thy answers, what but dark
> Ambiguous and with double sense deluding,
> Which they who asked have seldom understood,

---

[101] See Milton, *op. cit.*, p.448, ll.446-7n.

> And not well understood as good not known?
> Who ever by consulting at thy shrine
> Returned the wiser, or the more instruct
> To fly or follow what concerned him most,
> And run not sooner to his fatal snare?
> For God hath justly given the nations up
> To thy delusions; (I, 430-43)

Then, however, he grants the pagan prophets the occasional possibility of being right. This is not because Satan, their chief inspiration, could ever be right but because God could sometimes reveal the truth to them through the intervention of angels (as Aquinas explained in *Summa* II[102]). In any case we see that the heathens are denied all real power as natural truth-giving sources. For, in general, 'oracling' abuses the Gentiles and when it does not, it commits the sin of 'ascribing to itself' the truth 'foretold' (by the Christian God, that is). As a cure for this evil, Christ then presents himself as God's 'living oracle' who is accompanied by his 'spirit of truth' and this 'inward oracle', he declares, will henceforth provide 'all truth requisite for men to know'.

In Christ's reply to Satan's temptation of glory, we notice what at first seems to be a recognition of the value of heathen prophecy and truth. After giving the biblical example of Job, Christ points to Socrates as a 'memorable' martyr for the sake of truth:

> Poor Socrates (who next memorable?)
> By what he taught and suffered for so doing,
> For truth's sake suffering death unjust, lives now
> Equal in fame to proudest conquerors. (III, 96-99)

---

[102] *Ibid.*

But as B.K. Lewalski[103] indicates (in *Milton's Brief Epic*, Providence, 1966, p.240) this praise of Socrates derives from a tradition of commentary that considered Socrates' life and death as a herald of Christ's own. We realize therefore that Milton's chief motive in including Socrates here is a more conventionally Christian one than the juxtaposition of Socrates with Job may seem to indicate. Just as Job's patient worship in the face of suffering was a foreshadowing of Christ's more directly diabolical experiences in the desert (God himself refers to Job in this way in I, 147-49), so too Socrates' persecution and death for so-called sedition are a likeness of the last years of Christ's life. Besides it is not so much the nature of the truth (pagan, of course) which Socrates suffered for that is highlighted in Christ's commendation as the way in which Socrates' adherence to his cause (rather than to any hopes of 'fame and glory') elevates him far above a military conqueror like Scipio.

So far then, Christ exhibits a Christian view of truth which, while indifferently approving the life of a classical philosopher like Socrates, is nevertheless specifically condemnatory of all heathen claims to truth as those of devilish 'oracles'. This view attains its acutest development in the Great temptation of the '*vita contemplativa*' in Book IV. Having failed to seduce Christ with the attractions of riches, glory and political power, Satan finally decides to break his will with what he thinks must be Christ's greatest weakness, his addiction to 'contemplation and profound dispute'. This inference about Christ's intellectual pleasures he draws from the incident of the young Christ arguing with the Rabbis in the Temple (I, 210-14). But we the readers already know from Christ's musings in the first book that Satan's chances of success even here cannot be very strong

---

[103] See Milton, *op. cit.*, p.474, l.98n.

since the remembered event he bases this temptation on is one that Christ has already transcended in his spiritual maturity (1, 201-21)!

The precise manner in which Satan begins his temptation is strikingly similar to that employed in his seduction of Eve, with its major emphasis on extending the mind 'o'er all the world in knowledge':

> So let extend thy mind o'er all the world
> In knowledge, all things in it comprehend, (IV, 223-24)

Then, as if in bold reply to Raphael's and Michael's strong reliance on the Scriptures as the real source of knowledge and truth, Satan declares that

> All knowledge is not couched in Moses' law
> The Pentateuch or what the prophete wrote, (1V, 225-26)

Worse, he suggests that the pagans know and teach admirably because they are 'led by nature's light'. This, coming as it does from Satan's mouth, is a remarkable indication of the extent to which Milton's Christianity has now led him to criticize intellectualism, even of the Baconian, nature-based kind. The following section on the value of Gentile learning as a means of refuting non-Christian 'idolisms, traditions, paradoxes' is, as Schultz has pointed out, most probably a contribution to the learned ministry controversy:[104]

---

[104] See Schultz, *op. cit.*, p.227.

> And with the Gentiles much thou must converse,
> Ruling them by persuasion as thou mean'st,
> Without their learning how wilt thou with them,
> Or they with thee hold conversation meet?
> How wilt thou reason with them, how refute
> Their idolisms, traditions, paradoxes?
> Error by his own arms is best evinced. (1V,229-35)

As such this is another instance of Milton's persistent irritation against the prelates and presbyters of England. And, appropriately enough, the next line of Satan's subtly revives the second of the great hatreds that inspired so much of Milton's early writings, 'Look once more ere we leave this specular mount'. Though 'specular' is used by Milton mainly as 'affording an extensive view' it seems highly probable that one of Milton's reasons in coining this new word (the first recorded instance of it according to *OED*) was to include a slighting reference to 'speculations' and all the familiar institutions associated with this activity. (In fact Michael too at the end of his prophetic speech to Adam, says 'Let us descend now therefore from this top of speculation' [*Paradise Lost*, XII, 1.588], using 'speculation' with deliberate ambiguity.)

The particular classical glory Satan points to from this 'specular mount' is that of Athens, 'mother of arts and eloquence'. After a most agreeable description of the city with its 'studious walks and shades', groves and streams, Satan ventures to catalogue the ancient arts for which Greece was famous. He first notes the schools of the ancient sages and then the arts of music, and poetry. From there he proceeds to the 'lofty, grave' drama, and then on, finally, to oratory. After this preliminary look at the arts and eloquence of Greece comes the crucial eulogy of Greek philosophy. (ll.272-84) The first philosopher he acclaims is Socrates whom he describes as having brought philosophy down 'from heaven .... to the low-roofed house'. This is no doubt an allusion to Cicero's account of Socrates' preoccupation with moral questions rather than with scientific ones in his later life.[105] As such then Satan's picture of Socrates should be quite innocuous even to a Miltonic Christ. But unfortunately for Satan, there is in his peculiar phrasing of this feature of Socrates' thought, a blasphemous suggestion that Socrates' pagan philosophy is to be admired as *the* divinely inspired Truth in the place of 'Moses' law, the Pentateuch or what the prophets wrote'.[106] Satan goes on to describe Socrates as one who was recognized by the Delphic oracle ('well-inspired', he is careful to add) as 'wisest of men'. But this, we know, is scarcely likely to convince a man who has already cast the oracular authorities into a more than dubious position (I, 11.455-56). Satan then praises Socrates as the founder of several schools of philosophy including the 'Academics old and new, the Peripatetics, the Epicureans and the Stoics'. And in concluding his feat of intellectual salesmanship, he suggests that, by pursuing and possessing these various philosophies, Christ will become 'a king within thyself'. This reference to a kingdom within oneself is immediately recognizable as a perversion of Michael's benediction in Book XII, 1.585, where he assures Adam that deeds of faith, virtue, patience, temperance and love are the essential ingredients for an 'inner paradise'.

Having recognized thus so many associable weaknesses in Satan's admiration of the Greeks, we know, even before Christ begins his 'sage' reply, what that reply is going to contain. Only, there are some qualities in his manner of delivering this reply that shock us nevertheless. The first

---

[105] See Milton, *op. cit.*, p.502, 1.273n.

[106] See Carey in Milton, *op. cit.*, p.502, 1.273n for confirmation of this view.

sentence of Christ's speech is a characteristically Miltonic one:

> Think not but that I know these things, or think I know them not; (1V, 286-7)

Raphael employed the same technique in his astronomical dialogue in Book VIII (1.117 ff.) and now it is Christ's turn to similarly strengthen the credibility of his impending rejections by a declaration of superior intellectual awareness. Christ then goes on to qualify this statement rather radically by suggesting in his next clause that the knowledge he had admitted to at first is in effect valueless since it is not 'what I ought to know'. The reasons for its being of little worth are then elucidated by Christ (ll.288 ff.). The importance that Adam's angelic tutors, in so many different, indirect, ways placed on scriptural revelation as the source of all knowledge is now given its plainest and most uncompromising expression in Christ's words. Even if 'granted true' (a phrase that detracts considerably from his own earlier concession regarding the inspiration of oracles), all extra-scriptural doctrines are unnecessary ('No other doctrine needs') to one who is possessed of 'light from above'. In fact, they are 'false', 'little else but dreams', 'conjectures', 'fancies' and 'built on nothing firm'.

To substantiate this devastating remark Christ enters on a school by school rejection of Greek philosophy.[107] The first philosopher to be dismissed in Christ's increasingly bitter

---

[107] The method as Schultz has already explained, derives from a tradition '*contra paganos*' dating back to the Fathers. But even Schultz observes that these sermons on the pagans are not as one may see here the stuff of *Paradise Regained* and in context they appear less so. Neither Hakewill nor the Huguenot apologists Mornay and Amyhaut proclaimed scripture's sufficiency in Milton's angry voice' (Schultz, *op. cit.*, p.95).

diatribe is none other than Socrates. Having first described Socrates as the most memorable of men next to Job (1, 1.95) Christ now explodes the myth of his wisdom as really representing 'nothing':

> The first and wisest of them all professed
> To know this only, that he nothing knew (IV, 293-94)

The reason for this Christian superciliousness I have already indicated while considering Satan's presentation of Socratic wisdom in 11.273-74. The next on Christ's blacklist is Plato, whose entire intellectual system is simply summed up as consisting of 'fabling' and 'smooth conceits'. The Sceptics are then neatly described as those 'that doubted all things though plain sense'! By making Christ utter such naïveties, Milton not only betrays an extraordinary, even forced, insensitivity to the complexity of a school such as the Sceptics but also unconsciously exposes to attack the religious anti-naturalism that made him endorse Raphael's disregard for Adam's astronomical 'plain sense' in *Paradise Lost*, (see VIII,117-22 for example). Christ however proceeds with his harangue by laughing at the Peripatetics' concept of virtue:

> Others in virtue placed felicity,
> But virtue joined with riches and long life, (1V, 297-98)

Epicureanism is then denounced for placing all importance in 'corporal pleasure' and 'careless ease'.

The philosophers who come in for the most extended of Christ's criticisms however are the Stoics. For in the Stoics

Milton undoubtedly recognized all that was directly opposed to his own theocentric views of the value of the intellect:

> The Stoic last in philosophic pride,
> By him called virtue; (IV, 300-301)

The virtuous an according to the Stoics was 'perfect in himself'. Worse, he considered himself 'equal to God' this must have been, in Milton's eye, the most sinful of the dangers inherent in classical philosophy. So great in fact is Milton's hatred of the Stoics that he dismisses their transcendental philosophy with unholy haste as 'tedious talk', 'vain boasting' and 'subtle shifts conviction to evade', when in fact there is nothing morally exceptionable in most of the characteristics he indicates as constituting the actual philosophy of the Stoics:

> contemning all
> Wealth, pleasure, pain or torment,[108] death and life,
> Which when he lists, he leaves, or boasts he can,
> (IV,304-6)

As for the Stoics' attitude to 'death and life', I think it is significant that Milton more than once refers to it as 'boast'. It is certainly impossible to 'boast' of something that is totally insignificant. So that one cannot but feel that there is in Milton's strong rejection of Stoic philosophy even a lurking envy for their method of overcoming the sorrows of life and death. This shows us, I think, that apart from the exclusiveness of Milton's scriptural Christianity,

---

[108] In *De Doctrina Christiana* (Bk. 2, Ch. 10), Milton declares that stoical apathy is one of the opposites of 'true patience'. But the Biblical example of 'sensibility to pain' which he offers as the alternative to apathy is hardly adequate, since it is merely 'not inconsistent with true patience'!

another important reason for this elaborate critique of the ancients is his corollary obligation to refuse even some of the undeniably admirable qualities of the Greek philosophers.[109]

Christ's answer to the 'vain boast' of the Stoics is perhaps the weakest part of his speech. Almost crudely bending the argument in the 'tediously' familiar direction of 'self-knowledge' and 'God-knowledge', he declares:

> Alas what can they teach, and not mislead;
> Ignorant of themselves, of God much more, (1V, 309-10)

And then he goes on to insist that all the folly of 'the Stoics stems from their not knowing how the world began and how man fell degraded by himself, on grace depending'. This obsessional reliance on Scripture as the basis of all knowledge we have already met on several occasions in our survey of Milton's writings, but nowhere, I think, in such an awkwardly forced way. (Even Adam's clumsiness seems forgivable in comparison since he is at least an appealing little character whereas Christ himself is, to use Northop Frye's words, 'an uncreasingly unsympathetic figure, a pusillanimous quietist in the temptation of Parthia, an inhuman snob in the temptation of Rome, a

---

[109] This view is partly confirmed by Sensabaugh, (*op. cit.*, p.272.) 'Milton', he says, in accordance with theological dogma, could not allow anything good to come from the heathens'. He even goes so far as to suggest that, 'when Milton, through Christ, refused the wisdom of Greece and Rome, he refused it in name only; in reality he encompassed that wisdom'. While agreeing with Sensabaugh's view of Milton's recognition of the nature of classical wisdom, I think that Milton's refusal of this wisdom in *Paradise Regained* is more real than Sensabaughh suggests.

peevish obscurantist in the temptation of Athens'[110]). In fact, Christ's anger against those that in themselves seek virtue and to themselves all glory arrogate, to 'God give more' in 11.314-15 only adds to this effect of extraordinary querulousness. After a little further remonstration against the injustices done to his Father, Christ then declares:

> Who therefore seeks in these
> True wisdom, finds her not, or by delusion
> Far worse, her false resemblance only meets,
> An empty cloud. (III, 318-21)

It is important to note the reference to delusive wisdom in 11.319-20 for, in it, again, we have an inverted admission of the very real merit which Milton has no doubt detected in heathen philosophy and which he must now nonetheless condemn for its total lack of scriptural authorization.

The following section is a more surprising attack on books in general. The reason for this unnecessary extension of his denunciation of philosophy is apparently to emphasise the importance of 'spirit and judgement' in reading just as the twelfth verse of the twelfth chapter of Ecclesiastes does. But what it ultimately makes Christ do is to go to the extreme of suggesting: 'What he brings, what needs he elsewhere seek'. We see here that Milton's ever increasingly rigid

Protestantism has, after its various outbursts against science and knowledge and philosophy, finally ventured (even though in protective parenthesis) to discard all books in general because presumably they are all potentially dangerous to the Faith. This extremely narrow

---

[110] Frye, 'The Typology of 'Paradise Regained', *Modern Philology* 52-53, p.234.

manifestation of Christianity does seem to mark a change in the comparatively liberal views in *Areopagitica* which argued for the unlicensed printing of books in order to encourage intellectual debate. Though, as I indicated in my first chapter, the seeds of destruction are recognizable even there, in Milton's partial conception of Truth.[111] The reference to 'crude or *intoxicate*' which Christ makes in 1.328, incidentally, also reinforces my interpretation of the sin of Eve as a sin of knowledge since Eve's first reaction on eating the fruit was to feel 'heightened as with wine' effect that is now similarly attributed to much reading.

Having demolished all books, Christ then makes a vital literary concession that makes plain the reason for his contemptuous view of books. This concession is of course the Bible itself — chosen primarily because of its safeness as a source of knowledge. That the Bible is to be used as the answer to all the Satanic temptations of knowledge we have hitherto encountered in Milton is made clear by the diverse intellectual and educational virtues Christ commends in it. For music and for poetry, says Christ, the Scripture offers 'hymns', 'psalms' and 'Hebrew songs and harps', and then, in another access of pettishness, he adds that 'rather Greece from us these arts derived'. Not content with smearing its originality, Christ continues his denunciation of Greek literature in an Adam-like fashion (11.339-42). The features of the Greek's illimitation that he concentrates on reveal both Milton's puritanical disgust of pagan amorality and his continuing insistence (first seen in '*Of Education*') on utilitarian value as a requisite for all worthy literature. Besides, it offers little of 'delight' either: Greek songs are hopelessly inferior to those of Sion, because, in the latter, 'God is praised aright, and godlike men'. The reasons Milton gives for his rejection of heathen literature and art are, we

---

[111] See my 1st chapter.

are not astonished to note, the same as those that inspired all his other anti-intellectual attitudes. What is rather surprising about all these attitudes however is the growing vehemence with which Milton has been condemning all intellectual endeavour and learning that is not blessed by a scriptural 'fiat'. In the speech examined above, for instance, Christ rounds off his attack on Greek literature by basely insinuating that, as it is not inspired by the Christian God, it most probably is Satanic (1.350). However, he goes on to suggest (backed by the scriptural support of Romans 2, 14-15) that all is not 'quite lost' in the literature of the heathens if, with the help of the light of nature' (a token-concession to his own 'Baconianism'), it takes care to expound 'moral virtue'. This slight[112] extenuation of the Greeks' crimes against Christian morality and divinity, coming as it does after a long and vitriolic blast seems scarcely significant — especially when one links it up syntactically to ll.346-7 and discovers that all it really allows is a slight rise up the literary ladder on whose top rung the Bible is firmly ensconced.

Having annihilated Greek philosophy and literature, Christ finally turns to the oratorial magnificence that Satan has pointed out in Athens (ll.267-271). And, since it would be quite unimaginable to really appreciate anything at all in Satan's proffered gift of classical glory, he declares that they are

> herein to our prophets far beneath,
> As men divinely taught, and better teaching
> The solid rules of civil government
> In their majestic unaffected style
> Than all the oratory of Greece and Rome. (III, 356-60)

---

[112] Note the particular form in which Christ expresses it: 'not in all quite lost', with its many reluctant adverbs.

It has been pointed out by many critics including Stein (op. cit., p.95) and Samuel (op. cit., p.715) that one of the most objectionable features of Satan's presentation of Greece is its implications of the 'concept of mind as power' (Stein). But we only have to consider the way in which Christ refutes classical eloquence to realize that this is not entirely true. Christ's eulogy of 'our Law' and 'the prophets' is not a denial of the value of power (in this case stately power) but just an emphatic recommendation of the Bible as a better manual of civil government than the 'oratory of Greece and Rome':

> In them is plainest taught, and easiest learnt,
> What makes a nation happy, and keeps it so,
> What ruins kingdoms, and lays cities flat;
> These only with our Law best form a king. (III, 361-64)

Besides, it is scarcely likely that Milton could have considered financial and military power in nations as being quite sinful when in fact in *De Doctrina Christiana*, Bk. II, Ch. 17, he recommended obedience to God's commandments' because it 'makes nations prosperous in every respect.. It makes them fortunate, wealthy and victorious and lords over other nations'.[113] Satan, however, is by now, sufficiently frightened by Christ's fulminations to consider even his great temptation of the kingdoms of the mind as a failure and, so, he sensibly decides then to try more violent methods of destruction:

> Since neither wealth, nor honour, arms nor arts,
> Kingdom nor empire pleases thee, nor aught

---

[113] Milton, *Complete Prose Works*, edited by Wolfe and others, Vol. VI, p.804.

> By me proposed in life contemplative,
> Or active, tended on by glory, or fame,
> What dost thou in this world? The wilderness
> For thee is fittest place ... (III, 368-73)

~

The two most remarkable features of this intellectual temptation,[114] then, are the narrow scriptural basis on which Christ builds his argument against Greek philosophy, literature and oratory, and the extensive fury with which he utters it. The first feature we recognize as being merely the consummation of the increasingly single-minded adherence to the Scriptures, that provoked, first, the petulant outbursts against the Prelates and the Roman Catholics in the *Prolusions*, *Of Education* and *Areopagitica*, and, then, the dramatic-poetic attacks against scientific endeavour and knowledge in general in *Paradise Lost*. The second feature, though, is somewhat strange — not because Milton is less virulent in most of his other writings (virulence was a rhetorical feature he developed from the time of the Sixth Prolusion itself), but because the vehemence of Christ's speech has something of a desperate ring to it. Sensabaugh has suggested that it is probable that Milton changed his educational views

---

[114] Milton, as Carey (in Milton, *Complete Shorter Poems*, edited by Carey, p.503, 11.286-321n) points out, introduces this temptation into his interpretation of the Biblical account of Christ in the wilderness without precedent. This fact, coupled with the extraordinary length of Christ's attack and the very personal quality of his manner in delivering it, shows us that Milton certainly intended the rejection of Athens to be considered as much more than that of a 'dramatis personae', as Carey tries to suggest. In fact, as Samuel states, 'To be sure, Milton intended the entire action as generally applicable and the decisions made by Jesus as those every man should make'. (Samuel, *op. cit.*, p.715).

between the 1640s and the Restoration and that this explains the different ideals of *Of Education* and the epics. I think the changes in Milton's writings (changes that have more to do with tone than with content) are more subtle than a roughly twenty year historical period (however eventful) will allow. In this respect Samuel comes closer to the truth when she maintains that Milton's attitude to learning was in fact constant throughout his life. Only, she, like Stein and others, chooses to play-down the increasingly explicit anti-intellectualism in Milton's writings (explicit mainly through the tones employed) and stresses instead the all too obvious importance of the spirit and moral virtue in Milton's philosophy. The strident notes of Christ's volley in *Paradise Regained* do not, express merely a spiritual anger against Satanic immorality but, more interestingly, the very real fear of a Christian faced by various potentially anti-Christian features in the field of intellectual endeavour and education. It is this fear that both provokes the loud detonation of Athens and seeks, in an ultra-scholastic fashion, to set up Scriptural Doctrine and Truth as the only true need, spiritual and intellectual, of man. This extreme shrillness of tone therefore betrays not only Milton's Puritanical Christianity but also his growing awareness of the need to defend his strict doctrine against all extra-scriptural institutions. Milton, as one who was widely read in classical literature, just as he was certainly aware of the different trends of contemporary scientific enterprise, must no doubt have been alarmed by the threats these areas of human knowledge continually posed to Scriptural Faith. He therefore undertook upon himself, as a powerfully articulate Christian, first to spread the precepts of Protestantism safely among his fellowmen, then to justify the ways of God to men, and finally to prove the superiority of these ways to those of men. And in this gradually intensifying process of Christianisation Milton's original quasi-intellectualism was inevitably and inexorably transformed into a near-hysterical anti-intellectualism. That this transformation is really not a surprising one is what I have endeavoured to show by demonstrating the intellectual slightness of even the positive aspects of the *Prolusions, Of Education* and *Areopagitica*, (all commonly believed to be 'intellectually optimistic' works) and by stressing the continually anti-intellectual tones of *Paradise Lost* and *Paradise Regained*. An emotional fascination with one's own intelligence and reading is naturally not a lasting quality and an appreciation of the classics based largely on their utilitarian value is only too easily and wholly supplanted by the ethical utilitarianism of the Bible.

BIBLIOGRAPHY

Bacon, F. *Works*, Vol. 2, edited by Montagu, B. London, William Pickering, 1825.

Bundy, M. W. 'Milton's View of Education in Paradise Lost', *JEGP*, 21, 1922, 127-152.

Burden, D. H. *The Logical Epic*. London, Routledge and Kegan Paul, 1967.

Bush, D. *Paradise Lost in Our Time*. New York, Cornell University Press, 1945.

Bush, D. *English Literature in the Earlier Seventeenth Century 1600-1660*. Oxford, Clarendon Press, 1948.

Bush, D. *The Renaissance and English Humanism*. London, Oxford University Press, 1958.

Fletcher, H. F. *The Intellectual Development of John Milton*, 2 vols, Urbana, University of Illinois Press, 1961.

Frye, N. 'The Typology of Paradise Regained', *MP*, 52-53, 1954-1956, 227-238.

Grace, W. J. *Ideas in Milton*. Notre Dame, University of Notre Dame Press, 1968.

Hanford, J. H. 'The Temptation Motive in Milton', *SP*, 14-15, 1917-1918, 176-194.

Kelley, M. *This Great Argument*. Massachussetts, Peter Smith, 1962.

Lovejoy, A. O. 'Milton and the Paradox of the Fortunate Fall', *ELH*, 4, 1937, 161-179.

Lovejoy, A. O. 'Milton's Dialogue on Astronomy', in *Reason and the*

Imagination, edited by Mazzeo, J. A., London, Routledge and Kegan Paul, 1962, 129-142.

Mahood, M. M. *Poetry and Humanism*. London, Jonathan Cape, 1950.

McColley, G. 'Milton's Dialogue on Astronomy: The Principal Immediate Sources', *PMLA*, 52 i, 1937, 728-762.

Milton, J. *Complete Prose Works*, edited by Wolfe, D. M. and others, 6 vols, New Haven, Yale University Press, 1953-1973.

Milton, J. *Complete Shorter Poems*, edited by Carey, J. London, Longman, 1971.

Milton, J. *Paradise Lost*, edited by Fowler, A. London Longman, 1971.

Samuel, I. 'Milton on Learning and Wisdom', *PMLA*, 64i, 1949, 708-723.

Saurat, D. *Milton, Man and Thinker*. London, Jonathan Cape, 1925.

Schultz, H. *Milton and Forbidden Knowledge*. New York, Modern Language Association of America, 1955.

Sensabaugh, G. 'Milton on Learning', *SP*, 43, 1946, 258-272.

Steadman, J. N. 'Paradise Regained: Moral Dialectic and the Pattern of Rejection', *UTQ*, 31, 1961-1962, 416-427.

Stein, A. *Heroic Knowledge*. Connecticut, Archon Books, 1965.

Svendsen, K. *Milton and Science*, Cambridge, Harvard University Press, 1956.

Willey, B. *The Seventeenth Century Background*. Chatto and Windus, 1934.

www.ingramcontent.com/pod-product-compliance
Lightning Source LLC
LaVergne TN
LVHW051846080426
835512LV00018B/3102